WELFARE MAGNETS

WELFARE MAGNETS

A New Case for a National Standard

PAUL E. PETERSON
and
MARK C. ROM

The Brookings Institution
Washington, D.C.

Library of Congress Cataloging-in-Publication Data

Peterson, Paul E.
  Welfare magnets: a new case for a national standard/Paul E.
Peterson and Mark C. Rom, authors.
      p.   cm.
  Includes bibliographical references (p.   ) and index.
  ISBN 0-8157-7022-7   ISBN 0-8157-7021-9 (pbk.)
  1. Public welfare—United States.   2. Public welfare—
Wisconsin—Case studies.   3. Welfare recipients—United
States.   4. Welfare recipients—Wisconsin—Case studies.
I. Rom. Mark C., 1957–
II. Title.
HV95.P48   1990
362.5′09775—dc20   90-2653
                                                           CIP

9 8 7 6 5 4 3 2 1

THE BROOKINGS INSTITUTION

The Brookings Institution is an independent organization devoted to nonpartisan research, education, and publication in economics, government, foreign policy, and the social sciences generally. Its principal purposes are to aid in the development of sound public policies and to promote public understanding of issues of national importance.

The Institution was founded on December 8, 1927, to merge the activities of the Institute for Government Research, founded in 1916, the Institute of Economics, founded in 1922, and the Robert Brookings Graduate School of Economics and Government, founded in 1924.

The Board of Trustees is responsible for the general administration of the Institution, while the immediate direction of the policies, program, and staff is vested in the President, assisted by an advisory committee of the officers and staff. The by-laws of the Institution state: "It is the function of the Trustees to make possible the conduct of scientific research, and publication, under the most favorable conditions, and to safe-guard the independence of the research staff in the pursuit of their studies and in the publication of the results of such studies. It is not a part of their function to determine, control, or influence the conduct of particular investigations or the conclusions reached."

The President bears final responsibility for the decision to publish a manuscript as a Brookings book. In reaching his judgment on the competence, accuracy, and objectivity of each study, the President is advised by the director of the appropriate research program and weighs the views of a panel of expert outside readers who report to him in confidence on the quality of the work. Publication of a work signifies that it is deemed a competent treatment worthy of public consideration but does not imply endorsement of conclusions or recommendations.

The Institution maintains its position of neutrality on issues of public policy in order to safeguard the intellectual freedom of the staff. Hence interpretations or conclusions in Brookings publications should be understood to be solely those of the authors and should not be attributed to the Institution, to its trustees, officers, or other staff members, or to the organizations that support its research.

To
Margaret and Roy Rom
and to
the memory of
J. David Greenstone

Foreword

ALTHOUGH the federal government pays three-fourths of the cost of welfare assistance, the states set the benefit levels. As a consequence, the level of support among the states varies widely, more so than interstate disparities in wage rates or costs of living. This diversity in state welfare policies has created "welfare magnets"—states with comparatively high benefits that attract or retain the poor. The results are unfortunate, the authors of this study argue. States have substantially reduced benefit levels, poor families have been inhibited in their residential choices, and the employment opportunities of the poor have been unnecessarily restricted.

On the basis of their findings, Paul E. Peterson and Mark C. Rom recommend that the federal government establish a minimum national welfare standard to reduce the interstate variation in welfare benefits and reverse their overall decline. Under their proposal, welfare recipients would receive more uniform benefits in much the same way as other recipients of social insurance do. States' worries about becoming welfare magnets would be eased, while no state would have to pay a higher share of welfare costs than it currently pays.

Paul E. Peterson is the Henry Lee Shattuck Professor of Government at Harvard University. He directs the university's Center for American Political Studies and is former director of the Governmental Studies program at Brookings. Mark C. Rom, formerly a research fellow in the Brookings Governmental Studies program, is a social science analyst at the General Accounting Office.

The authors wish to thank the following people who gave valuable

comments on portions of the manuscript: Rebecca M. Blank, Gary
T. Burtless, John E. Chubb, Russell Hanson, John Kincaid, Gary
King, Robert Meyer, Gary Miller, Robert Reischauer, William Riker,
Lester Salamon, Jules Sugarman, R. Kent Weaver, Margaret Weir,
Joseph White, and Richard F. Winters. They are also grateful to
the following for research assistance: Mark B. Arnold, Jeffrey
Binder, Eric Boyd, David F. Godshalk, Jessica Korn, Robert Lie-
berman, Maria Mitchell, and Patrick Wolf.

Nancy D. Davidson edited the manuscript. Renuka D. Deonarain,
Barbara Johnson, Vida R. Megahed, Eloise Stinger, and Eje Wray
helped in the preparation of numerous drafts of the manuscript.
Linda Keefer verified its factual content, Susan L. Woollen prepared
it for typesetting, and Max Franke prepared the index.

Financial assistance was provided by the Joseph B. Grossman
Fund of the Center for American Political Studies at Harvard
University and the Center for the Study of American Government
at Johns Hopkins University. An earlier version of chapter 3
appeared in the September 1989 *American Political Science Review.*

The interpretations, conclusions, and recommendations presented
here are solely those of the authors and should not be ascribed to
the persons whose assistance is acknowledged, to any agency that
funded research, to the U.S. General Accounting Office, or to the
trustees, officers, or other staff members of the Brookings Institution.

BRUCE K. MACLAURY
President

September 1990
Washington, D.C.

Contents

Appendixes

Figures

Tables

Chapter 1

Is There a Problem?

POLITICIANS seldom advocate more money for poor people. The image that comes to mind is of lazy, disheveled welfare recipients lounging about unkempt, crime-ridden, drug-infested housing projects overrun with undisciplined children. More money, it is believed, will do more harm than good. More money, it is argued, entrenches deep-seated patterns of behavior, perpetuates a cycle of indolence and misery, and reinforces a culture of poverty. And yet politicians seldom propose cuts in aid to the poor. They resist being portrayed as the Scrooge who denies starving families the pittance they need to keep alive.

The best way of handling the question of how much to give the poor, politicians have discovered, is to avoid doing anything about it at all. As a result, a consensus on welfare reform emerged in the late 1980s that neatly skirted a number of difficult questions, all relating to money: How large should welfare benefits be? Who should pay for them? Should benefits be uniform throughout the country? Or should they vary from state to state?

Instead of addressing these questions, consensus was reached by appealing to the values of work and family, which have universal appeal. It was agreed that education and job training should be provided so that welfare recipients could acquire the skills needed to become active members of the work force, that day care and medical insurance should be made available to recipients who found employment, and that assiduous efforts should be made to get fathers to pay child support if they left their families.[1]

---

1. The extent of the consensus on welfare should not be exaggerated, of course. Although most agreed that job training was needed, some favored the program

1

Agreement on these issues was widespread enough that Congress was able to pass the Family Support Act of 1988, the first welfare reform legislation enacted in decades. The act embraced the values of work and family by setting up job training programs, funding child care and medical services, extending aid to two-parent families, and tightening child support laws. Yet these provisions, for all their merit, have not greatly reduced the need for welfare assistance. Only 20 percent of welfare recipients will even be enrolled in job programs. And the best evidence available as to these programs' efficacy suggests that they will only slightly increase the rate of employment. More vigorous enforcement of child support provisions is expected to remove less than 200,000 families from the welfare rolls. Millions more will remain in need of public assistance. Thus there remains the difficult question of money—the amount that the government decides is the minimum people need in order to live decently.

That issue is so difficult that federal policymakers have never been able to resolve it. In the fifty years since the program of aid to families with dependent children (AFDC) was established, Congress has at no time decided on the appropriate level of support for welfare recipients. Despite the fact that Congress foots more than half the AFDC bill, it has left this crucial question to the predilections of state legislatures.

---

because they thought that most people on welfare wanted to work and would accept a job or the training necessary to obtain a job, if only it were available. These analysts believed that voluntary job training programs were the most successful, and they also called for programs of public employment that provided work for those who could not otherwise obtain a job. See William Julius Wilson, *The Truly Disadvantaged: The Inner City, the Underclass, and Public Policy* (University of Chicago Press, 1987). Others were less sure that welfare recipients were eager to secure employment. See Lawrence M. Mead, *Beyond Entitlement: The Social Obligations of Citizenship* (Free Press, 1986). In their view, those on the dole had to be forced to accept employment as a condition of financial support. Otherwise, the rigors of low-wage employment—regular attendance, willingness to do dull or repetitive tasks, orders by an unpleasant boss, quarrels with fellow employees—would lead to early resignations or dismissals. Unless recipients were made to work, they were never likely to acquire the habits, self-discipline, and skills necessary to move beyond such low-wage jobs.

Who Should Determine Welfare Policy?

The issue has not been left to the states simply by default. On the contrary, it has been debated regularly since the social welfare system was created during the New Deal. One of the most ambitious efforts to move toward the creation of a national standard was made in 1969 by President Richard Nixon as part of his family assistance plan (FAP). Legislation enacting the plan passed the House of Representatives but died in the Senate Finance Committee in the face of intense conservative criticism and waning liberal support. President Jimmy Carter's attempts to reform welfare also called for more uniform policies among the states, but once again the proposals passed by the House were buried in the Senate Finance Committee.

Instead of building on the recommendations of its predecessors, the Reagan administration advocated moving in the opposite direction. In 1982 it proposed a new federalism in which the states would assume complete fiscal responsibility for welfare policy. When that proposal failed to win either congressional or gubernatorial support, the administration issued a report in 1986 that continued to urge greater state control of welfare policy, arguing that "our centralized welfare system contribute[s] significantly to the persistence of poverty in America." Because the administration believed that no one—least of all the federal government—knows the solutions to the nation's complicated poverty problem, it recommended initiating "a program of widespread, long-term experiments in welfare policy through state-sponsored and community-based demonstration projects. . . . Congress should seek . . . legislation that would waive federal welfare rules in order to allow states and communities to experiment."[2]

But if the Reagan administration believed further decentralization was necessary, other reformers took an opposing point of view. The National Governors' Association and the American Public

2. *Up from Dependency: A New National Public Assistance Strategy,* Report to the President by the Domestic Policy Council, Low Income Opportunity Working Group (Government Printing Office, December 1986), p. 3.

Welfare Association (composed of the chief welfare administrator in each state), while agreeing that states needed flexibility on work requirements and other administrative questions, called for clearer national benefit standards, including "a new cash assistance program based on a national formula reflecting the actual cost of living within each state." They proposed that a consistent percentage of each state's family living standard be paid jointly by the federal and state government.[3] Two years later, a Ford Foundation panel argued that "a national minimum benefit equal to two-thirds of the Federal poverty level . . . is an achievable goal for the early 1990s."[4] The rationale for proposals of this type was given by Senator Daniel J. Evans, who served as cochairman of the Committee on Federalism and National Purpose of the National Conference on Social Welfare: "At the national level there needs to be a safety net for our citizens. . . . [We should] assume this fiscal responsibility at the federal level. . . . [and] create broader, more uniform welfare support. . . . [This] will eventually result in reducing the number of poor people."[5]

These policy debates echo a similar debate within the scholarly community. Some have argued that states should be allowed to set welfare levels, because this increases the number of combinations of taxing and spending available; citizens can then choose to live in states whose policies best match their policy preferences.[6] Others have replied that if states bear the responsibility for redistributive programs each state will limit its welfare provision, hoping that some other government will take care of the poor.[7]

3. John Herbers, "Governors Urge Tying Welfare Benefits to Jobs," *New York Times,* February 18, 1987, p. A15.

4. Executive Panel of the Ford Foundation Project on Social Welfare and the American Future, *The Common Good: Social Welfare and the American Future* (New York: Ford Foundation, 1989), p. 63.

5. Office of Senator Daniel J. Evans, "Federalism Press Briefing," October 2, 1986.

6. Mark V. Pauly, "Income Redistribution as a Local Public Good," *Journal of Public Economics,* vol. 2 (February 1973), pp. 35–58; and Charles M. Tiebout, "A Pure Theory of Local Expenditures," *Journal of Political Economy,* vol. 64 (October 1956), pp. 416–24.

7. Charles C. Brown and Wallace E. Oates, "Assistance to the Poor in a Federal System," University of Maryland, Department of Economics, 1986; Helen F. Ladd

This debate actually hinges on two empirical issues. The first concerns the effect of welfare policy on residential choices. Some have found that welfare policies have little influence on individuals' decisions about where to live and that people migrate (or remain at home) mainly for reasons of family or job opportunities.[8] Other studies find evidence that states offering higher welfare benefit levels act as a magnet by both attracting poor people who would not otherwise move there and by retaining poor people who might otherwise choose to leave.[9]

The second issue concerns how states determine their welfare policies. The dominant approach to state policymaking holds (often implicitly) that politicians respond exclusively to political forces within their states.[10] A contrasting approach emphasizes that states are engaged in economic competition and that policymakers establish policies to enhance their state's economic position.[11] As a result, forces external to the state help shape a state's policies, requiring it to focus on developmental strategies and deemphasize redistributive programs.

The data that we shall present in this book provide answers to both these questions. We show that the residential choices of poor people are influenced not only by job opportunities and prospective wages but also by the level of welfare benefits available in a state.

and Fred C. Doolittle, "Which Level of Government Should Assist the Poor?" *National Tax Journal*, vol. 35 (September 1982), pp. 323–36; and Paul E. Peterson, *City Limits* (University of Chicago Press, 1981).

8. Gary S. Fields, "Place-to-Place Migration: Some New Evidence," *Review of Economics and Statistics*, vol. 61 (February 1979), pp. 21–32; and Larry H. Long, "Poverty Status and Receipt of Welfare among Migrants and Nonmigrants in Large Cities," *American Sociological Review*, vol. 39 (February 1974), pp. 46–56.

9. Rebecca M. Blank, "The Impact of State Economic Differentials on Household Welfare and Labor Force Behavior," *Journal of Public Economics*, vol. 28 (October 1985), pp. 25–58; and Edward M. Gramlich and Deborah S. Laren, "Migration and Income Redistribution Responsibilities," *Journal of Human Resources*, vol. 19 (Fall 1984), pp. 489–511.

10. Edward T. Jennings, Jr., "Competition, Constituencies, and Welfare Policies in American States," *American Political Science Review*, vol. 73 (June 1979), pp. 414–29; and Robert D. Plotnick and Richard F. Winters, "A Politico-Economic Theory of Income Redistribution," *American Political Science Review*, vol. 79 (June 1985), pp. 458–73.

11. Peterson, *City Limits*; and Wallace E. Oates, *Fiscal Federalism* (Harcourt, Brace, Jovanovich, 1972).

We also find that states take into account their competitive relationships with other states when setting their welfare policies. They
lower their benefits when their benefits are comparatively high,
and they also lower their benefits when the percentage of poor
people in the state increases. These findings lead us to the conclusion
that the federal government, not the states, is the appropriate locus
for determining welfare assistance levels.

Federal assumption of this responsibility would mark a significant
change in U.S. welfare policy. Still, there has been a steady shift
in responsibility from the state to the national government in
welfare policy over the course of the twentieth century. The Family
Support Act of 1988 represents a further step in this direction. It
imposes on states, for the first time, the requirements that they
withhold court-ordered child support payments from the wages of
absent parents, provide benefits to needy two-person families for at
least six months a year, establish work and training programs, and
provide financial assistance to ease the transition to work. Setting
a national welfare standard would only be another step forward
along a path toward a national welfare policy that the nation has
been traveling on for many decades.

The Current Welfare Policymaking System

The social welfare system in the United States, as embodied in
the Social Security Act of 1935, contains four basic income support
programs.[12] Social security is the largest and most universal,
providing pensions to approximately 34 million elderly persons.
Almost all Americans anticipate receiving social security benefits
upon their retirement. Unemployment compensation is nearly as
universal a program; it helps protect as many as 90 million American
workers from the loss of income due to involuntary unemployment,
though only a small fraction of these workers receive benefits at

12. In addition, there are programs that provide noncash benefit programs, such
as medicaid, medicare, food stamps, and various housing programs. The only noncash
program that will be considered in this study is food stamps; unlike the others, the
cash value of the food stamps to the recipient can be readily calculated and is roughly
equivalent to their face value.

any one time. Supplemental security income (SSI) provides coverage to a more limited set of Americans: it dispenses benefits to 4 million blind, disabled, and elderly persons not adequately covered by social security retirement insurance. Aid to families with dependent children, the most controversial of the income support programs and the one commonly known as "welfare," provides income support to about 15 million Americans in families where the father (or principal wage earner) has died, is unemployed but not receiving unemployment benefits, or is otherwise absent from the home. It is this program that is the central concern of this book.

States set the benefit levels for AFDC in a roundabout way. First they calculate a "needs standard," which is regarded as the amount necessary for a family to buy a reasonable amount of food, clothing, and shelter. Any family whose income is below the needs standard and is otherwise eligible can receive assistance. The state then decides the maximum amount it will provide eligible families by determining what percentage of the needs standard it will supply. The actual grant is the difference between this maximum amount and the amount of income the family earns, disregarding a certain amount for child care costs, transportation costs, and, for a period of time, a percentage of the income the recipient has earned.

States differ in their assessment of what a family needs to meet a reasonable standard of living. They also differ in the percentage of that standard they are willing to pay to help a family meet its needs. Taken together, the disparity in judgment among the states is quite remarkable. California, the most generous of the forty-eight contiguous states, provided welfare recipients in 1990 with an AFDC stipend nearly six times as large as that provided by Alabama, the least generous state. The maximum welfare benefit paid to a California family of three was $694 a month, compared with $118 paid to a similar family in Alabama.[13]

These policy differences among the states are not just the peculiarities of one or two states, nor are they gradually disappearing as state governments gain in professional responsibility and fiscal capacity. Instead, as can be seen in table 1-1, benefits varied as

13. *Overview of Entitlement Programs,* Committee Print, House Committee on Ways and Means, 101 Cong. 2 sess. (GPO, 1990), p. 556.

TABLE 1-1. Interstate Variations in Welfare Benefits, Selected Years, 1940–90[a]
Amounts in 1985 dollars

Benefit	1940		1950		1960		1970		1975		1980		1985		1990	
	Mean amount	Vari-ation	Mean amount	Vari-ation	Mean amount	Vari-ation	Mean amount	Vari-ation	Mean amount	Vari-ation	Mean amount	Vari-ation	Mean amount	Vari-ation	Mean amount	Vari-ation
Average monthly AFDC payment	228	0.33	319	0.34	394	0.32	450	0.34	381	0.35	319	0.34	292	0.35	285[b]	0.35
Maximum monthly AFDC payment																
3-person family	n.a.	n.a.	n.a.	n.a.	n.a.	n.a.	n.a.	n.a.	462	0.33	388	0.34	326	0.34	315	0.37
4-person family	n.a.	n.a.	n.a.	n.a.	610	0.34	597	0.36	542	0.34	449	0.36	389	0.33	372	0.36
Maximum combined AFDC/food stamp payments																
3-person family	c	c	c	c	c	c	n.a.	n.a.	670	0.19	576	0.19	526	0.18	511	0.18
4-person family	c	c	c	c	c	c	740	0.21	812	0.19	694	0.19	647	0.17	613	0.16

Sources: Authors' calculations based on Department of Health and Human Services, Office of Family Assistance, Division of Research, Evaluation, and Statistics, State Data and Program Characteristics Branch, "Flash Report," SSA-3635, December 1986; HHS, Family Support Administration, Office of Family Assistance, Characteristics of State Plans for AFDC, 1986, p. 85; Social Security Administration, Social Security Bulletin, vol. 50 (January 1987), pp. 76–77; Bureau of the Census, Statistical Abstract of the United States: 1941, 63d ed. (Department of Commerce, 1942), p. 410; 1951, 72d ed. (1951), p. 247; 1961, 82d ed. (1961), p. 287; 1975, 96th ed. (1975), p. 345; 1981, 102d ed. (1981), pp. 306, 344, 345; Department of Health, Education, and Welfare, pub. SRS 78-03200, ORS report, July 1975, pp. 8, 9; Social Security Administration, pub. 13-11924, ORS D-2, February 1980, p. 10; Fed. Reg. 80-17597, 85-21339; and Overview of Entitlement Programs, Committee Print, House Committee on Ways and Means, 101 Cong. 2 sess. (Government Printing Office, 1990), p. 965.

n.a. Not available.
a. Variations are coefficients of variation (standard deviation divided by mean).
b. As of 1989.
c. Food stamps not generally available before 1975.

much in 1990 as they did in 1940. A statistical measure of variability that allows for comparisons across time is the coefficient of variation (the standard deviation divided by the mean). It has not only remained remarkably stable over the entire period, but its average size—0.34—indicates a substantial degree of interstate variation. Roughly speaking, a comparatively generous state is providing nearly $300 a month more for a family of three than a comparatively frugal state.[14]

This variability in benefit levels has persisted even though the value of welfare benefits in real dollars has been declining since 1970. After rising steadily throughout the early postwar period, both maximum and average benefit levels in inflation-adjusted dollars have declined steadily so that benefit levels in the typical state were in 1990 only two-thirds of what they were in 1970 and were lower than they had been since 1950 (see table 1-1).

States also differ in the requirements an applicant must meet in order to be eligible for welfare assistance. They decide such questions as the amount of assets a recipient can retain and still remain eligible for benefits, the number of days that can elapse between the time an application is made and an eligibility decision is reached, and the age at which a child can no longer be counted as a member of the eligible family. In 1985 there were at least thirty-two significant regulations affecting welfare eligibility that varied from state to state. Not surprisingly, it was easier to gain access to the welfare rolls of the states with the more generous benefits.[15]

The food stamp program, for which the federal government both provides funds and establishes benefit levels, has reduced the interstate variation in combined total benefits by roughly one-half, compared with the variation in the period before food stamps were

14. A comparatively generous state is defined as a state one standard deviation above the mean; a frugal state is one standard deviation below.

15. On an eligibility permissiveness index, with a scale from 0 (restrictive) to 100 (permissive), the average state scored 47, with the most restrictive state scoring 28 and the most permissive scoring 75. In 1985 the eligibility permissiveness index had a 0.67 correlation with benefit levels. Paul E. Peterson and Mark C. Rom, "The Case for a National Welfare Standard," *Brookings Review*, vol. 6 (Winter 1988), pp. 24–32.

introduced (see table 1-1). This occurs because recipients in states with lower cash benefits receive more food stamps. For every three-dollar difference in cash benefits, food stamp benefits increase by about one dollar. However, combined food stamp and cash benefits in the most generous of the contiguous states still remain over twice as high as in the least: the highest combined benefits for a family of three are $832 a month, the lowest, $378.[16]

The food stamp program has also tempered the decline in welfare benefits. If food stamp coupons are counted as equivalent to cash, then welfare benefits did not fall by all that much between 1960 and 1985. Food stamp and cash payments in 1990 were roughly the same as cash payments were in 1968, when the food stamp program had yet to be inaugurated.[17] But if the food stamp program seems to have offset the decline in cash benefits, it may also be the case that giving more food stamp benefits to recipients in states with lower cash benefits discourages states from funding their cash assistance programs. In fact, it may well be argued that food stamps, originally thought to be an addition to cash benefits, have become a substitute instead.[18] As federal contributions in the form of food stamps have increased, cash benefit levels set by states have fallen by a corresponding amount. The political mechanisms by which this has taken place are discussed in chapter 4.

16. *Overview of Entitlement Programs,* Committee Print, pp. 553–54. Congress has set a national maximum food stamp amount, which in 1990 was $260 a month for a three-person family. This amount is adjusted for each state depending upon the state's maximum AFDC benefits and certain other deductions. The formula for calculating food stamps causes food stamp benefits to increase by thirty cents whenever cash benefits are reduced by one dollar and to decline by thirty cents whenever cash benefits are increased by one dollar. *Overview of Entitlement Programs,* Committee Print, pp. 1263, 1264.

17. Maximum AFDC benefits for a family of four in the average state were $660 in 1968; combined maximum AFDC and food stamp benefits for the same size family were $645 in 1990. (Both figures are in 1985 dollars.) Calculated from *Overview of Entitlement Programs,* Committee Print, p. 965.

18. Robert Moffitt, "Has State Redistribution Policy Grown More Conservative? AFDC, Food Stamps and Medicaid, 1960–1984," Discussion Paper 851-88 (University of Wisconsin, Institute for Research on Poverty, January 1988).

Differences in Cost of Living and Wages

It might be thought that welfare benefits vary because the cost of living varies from state to state. To ascertain whether this was the case, we estimated the cost of living for forty-two states by using data on the cost of living in 300 cities.[19] In both 1980 and 1985 all but five of the states had a cost of living within 10 percent of the national average. Even the state with the highest cost of living—Massachusetts—had costs that were only 38 percent higher than the costs in Kentucky, the least expensive state in 1980, and 44 percent higher than costs in Arkansas, the least expensive state in 1985. When all states are considered together, the variation in AFDC benefits is four times larger than the variation in the cost of living. The combined AFDC and food stamp benefit varies twice as much as the cost of living (table 1-2).

Wages also fluctuate from state to state. Perhaps state officials set welfare benefits below local wage rates, so that one can always earn more by working than by receiving welfare. But this is an unlikely explanation for the interstate variation in benefits, because a national minimum wage has made the pay for low-wage jobs the same in both California and Mississippi. Although some occupations, most notably in agricultural and small retail trade establishments, are exempted from the minimum wage and some employers do not comply with minimum wage legislation, 83 percent of all nonsupervisory jobs in the private, nonagricultural sector were covered by the basic federal minimum wage in 1976. State minimum wage laws extended this coverage to another 8 percent of the work force, so that "combined coverage in 1976 included 90 percent of all nonsupervisory workers." All but 2 percent of the fully employed

19. American Chamber of Commerce Researchers Association, *Inter-City Cost of Living Indicators* (Indianapolis: ACCRA, 1980, 1985). To obtain an estimate of a state's cost of living, we calculated the average of the cost of living of all the cities within the state, weighted by the size of each city's population. This estimate of interstate costs of living is, of course, limited to urban areas; it does not take into account differences in the cost of living between rural and urban areas within states. But neither do most state welfare benefit levels.

TABLE 1-2. Interstate Variations in Welfare Programs, Wages, and Cost of Living, 1985

Program	Coefficient of variation
Aid to families with dependent children	0.34
Aid to families with dependent children and food stamps[a]	0.18
Social security retirement	0.00[b]
Supplemental security insurance[c,d]	0.13
Supplemental security insurance and food stamps[c]	0.08
Unemployment compensation[e]	0.17
Unemployment compensation and food stamps[e]	0.10
Cost of living	0.08
Average manufacturing wages	0.14
Federal minimum wage	0.00[b]

Source: *Background Material and Data on Programs within the Jurisdiction of the Committee on Ways and Means*, Committee Print, House Committee on Ways and Means, 100 Cong. 2 sess. (Government Printing Office, 1988), pp. 312–13, 371–72, 471–72; American Chamber of Commerce Researchers Association, *Inter-City Cost of Living Indicators* (Indianapolis: ACCRA, 1985); and Department of Labor, Bureau of Labor Statistics, *Handbook of Labor Statistics* (December 1985), pp. 218–19.

a. Maximum benefit for a three-person family.
b. Social security benefits and federal minimum wage are uniform across the states.
c. Data are for 1986.
d. Maximum benefit for a two-person family.
e. Maximum benefit for worker receiving unemployment compensation.

adult males were working for wages at or above the legal minimum in 1973 and 1975.[20] By 1984 this had declined to 1 percent.[21] Furthermore, the actual variation in wages among the states appears to be substantially less than the variation in welfare benefits. Unfortunately, no data on average wages for all jobs are available by state, so we used the average wages in the manufacturing sector in making our calculations. Even manufacturing wages, which could be expected to differ greatly among states, vary by less than half

20. Finis Welch, *Minimum Wages: Issues and Evidence* (Washington: American Enterprise Institute for Public Policy Research, 1978), pp. 3, 6; and Edward M. Gramlich, "Impact of Minimum Wages on Other Wages, Employment and Family Incomes," *Brookings Papers on Economic Activity, 1976:2*, p. 421.

21. We calculated this percentage from information reported in Richard V. Burkhauser and T. Aldrich Finegan, "The Minimum Wage and the Poor: The End of a Relationship," *Journal of Policy Analysis and Management*, vol. 8 (Winter 1989), p. 58. Their estimate is for workers between the ages of 17 and 64.

as much as AFDC benefits (table 1-2). It is hard to conclude that welfare benefits need to vary as much as they do to match prevailing wages.

Advantages for the Poor of a National Standard

Since interstate differences in wage levels or the cost of living neither account for nor adequately justify the differentials in welfare benefits, it is worth considering whether it would not be better public policy if such benefits were standardized throughout the United States. One benefit to the poor of a uniform welfare standard can hardly be disputed. If the poor and the welfare dependent knew that benefits remained the same wherever they lived, they could move freely from one state to another whenever such a move seemed necessary to reunite a family, search for a job, make a clean break with the past, or in some other way improve their situation. If program administration as well as benefits were standardized, the poor and the welfare dependent could avoid the high costs of reconnecting to the welfare bureaucracy with each interstate move they made.

The advantages of having the federal government establish and administer benefits become clear when one considers the social security program serving the elderly. Social security benefits do not vary from one part of the United States to another. Nor is it difficult to continue to receive these benefits if one moves temporarily or permanently to a different state. Adjustments are not made for interstate differences in cost of living, cost of medical services, or wage levels. Benefits can be received not only in any of the fifty states but overseas as well. As a result, the retired population is surprisingly mobile; it moves to Florida, Arizona, Texas, Hawaii, and Mexico. But it is not just sunshine and the relaxed life of retirement colonies that attract the elderly. Many move to be near their sons, daughters, and grandchildren, and such moves can be from any state to any other. Were social security benefits tied to a particular location, were they to vary dramatically from one part of the United States to another, and were it necessary to go through a lengthy bureaucratic process to renew benefits each time an interstate move was made, a practice considered normal and desirable would have been sharply curtailed.

Those who receive supplemental security income—the blind, deaf, disabled, and elderly not eligible for more than minimal social security benefits—receive benefits that vary from one state to another, but the amount of variation is less than one-half the amount of variation in the AFDC program (table 1-2). In 1990 maximum SSI benefit levels for an individual with no other income ranged from $386 to $752 a month; when augmented with food stamps, benefits in the lowest states rose to $458.[22] SSI benefits are relatively uniform because in 1972 the federal government mandated and funded a national minimum. Not only do SSI benefits vary less, but, in contrast with AFDC, they have risen steadily with increases in the cost of living. The federal share of SSI benefits is adjusted for inflation the same way that social security benefits are.

The unemployment compensation program, while subject to state determination of benefit levels, is funded by a uniform tax that does not vary among states. This prevents states from trying to attract firms by lowering their unemployment compensation taxes. Since there is no national minimum, there is more variation in unemployment compensation benefit levels than in SSI levels.[23] But since the tax rate for the fund from which unemployment benefits are drawn is uniform, the variation in benefits is substantially less than the variation in AFDC benefits (table 1-2). Variation in

22. The low figure is for the twenty-four states that do not supplement the federal minimum. The high is for Connecticut. In Alaska benefits were $717 a month, but we have excluded this state and Hawaii from all of our analyses. *Overview of Entitlement Programs,* Committee Print, p. 709.

23. Compared with 0.08 for SSI combined with food stamps, the coefficient of variation for unemployment compensation was 0.12 in 1975, 0.13 in 1980, 0.15 in 1985, and 0.17 in 1988. These coefficients of variation are for the average weekly benefit paid to an unemployed person in the years indicated in the text. Calculated from data in *Social Security Bulletin,* vol. 38 (November 1975), table M-37, p. 64; vol. 43 (December 1980), table M-38, p. 68; vol. 49 (April 1986), table M-35, p. 55; and vol. 52 (May 1989), table M-33, p. 68. The coefficient of variation for state wage replacement rates of wages by unemployment insurance for 1964–81 was 0.14. Calculated from data reported in Walter Corson, Alan Hershey, and Stuart Kerachsky, *Nonmonetary Eligibility in State Unemployment Insurance Programs: Law and Practice* (Kalamazoo, Mich.: W. E. Upjohn Institute for Employment Research, 1986), p. 31.

unemployment benefits is less because states realize that businesses within their states are paying at the same tax rate into the unemployment compensation fund as businesses in other states. Higher benefits within the state do not contribute immediately and directly into higher states taxes, and, if a state's benefit levels are too much lower than those in other states, then state tax dollars are merely siphoned off to other states.

Although the advantages of a national system for AFDC would seem to be at least as great as the advantages of the more uniform policies for the social security, SSI, and unemployment compensation programs, groups claiming to represent the poor—most notably the National Welfare Rights Organization (NWRO)—have at times argued against a national minimum benefit. When President Nixon proposed to establish a national minimum in the early 1970s, the NWRO opposed it because they saw this benefit as inadequate. They also fought the plan because they feared that states currently offering higher benefits (such as New York, where many NWRO members lived) would cut their benefits back if a lower minimum standard was approved nationally (see chapter 4).

The NWRO miscalculated in two ways. First, it advocated a national standard that was more than three times that proposed by the president, a misreading of what was politically possible. Moreover, in opposing a national standard for fear that it would lower benefits in New York, the NWRO failed to take into account the likelihood that variable state benefits would in the long run also depress benefits in New York and other high-benefit states.

States are more prone than the federal government to provide inadequate benefits for both political and economic reasons. Briefly, the process that depresses state-determined benefit levels works as follows. Government officials in states with high benefit levels perceive that poor people are migrating into their state, apparently in response to their relatively high welfare benefits. The more the state does for its needy, the more needy people it attracts from throughout the country, and the higher the percentage of poverty the state suffers. The increase in the number of poor people in the state places a higher demand on public services. States are faced with the unhappy prospect of either cutting services back or raising taxes to pay for them. Higher taxes generate not only political opposition but also the economically disturbing possibility that businesses and prosperous residents might move to other states to lower their costs.

These changes do not happen overnight, of course. And the political repercussions are more likely to surface long before the economic consequences become apparent. People raise their voices in opposition first; they exit from the community only after they conclude that their political complaints are ineffective. But if government leaders are shrewd politicians, and they often are, then they can learn to read the writing on the wall even when the lettering is faint and the symbols are hard to interpret.

The suggestion that the poor move to places where benefits are high can be subject to sharp dispute. Especially during political campaigns, the charges and countercharges can misrepresent the actual condition existing at any given time. On the one side, it is often claimed that welfare recipients are too poor to move any considerable distance or that they ignore benefit levels when choosing their place of residence. On the other side, it is claimed that the poor are flocking into the state in large numbers while taxpayers and businesses are fleeing. The truth is very likely to be more complex: many factors affect the residential choices of both families and firms, and welfare policies and tax rates are just two of these many factors.

As to the geographical mobility of the poor, there can be little doubt. A substantially higher percentage of poor than nonpoor households moved across state lines between 1976 and 1980 and again between 1981 and 1985: 13 percent versus 11 percent in the first period and 15 percent versus 10 percent in the second. The trend continued between 1986 and 1987, when 5 percent of poor households migrated to another state, compared with 3 percent of the nonpoor.[24] The white poor and the poor living outside the South

24. Bureau of the Census, "Geographical Mobility: March 1975 to March 1980," *Current Population Reports,* series P-20, no. 368 (Department of Commerce, 1981), table 36, p. 101; table 40, p. 125; "March 1980 to March 1981," no. 377 (1983), table 36, p. 102; table 40, p. 126; "1985," no. 420 (1987), table 12, p. 37; table 19, pp. 51–52; "March 1986 to March 1987," no. 430 (1989), table 36, p. 88; table 40, p. 100; and Bureau of the Census, *Statistical Abstract of the United States: 1987,* 107th ed. (Department of Commerce, 1986), table 753, p. 446.

are especially likely to move, compared with their nonpoor counterparts (see table 1-3). But poor blacks and poor southerners are just about as mobile as nonpoor blacks and southerners.

The greater mobility of the poor is not a recent phenomenon.[25] But the greater long distance mobility of welfare recipients is. Between 1968 and 1971 the interstate mobility of younger families with female heads receiving welfare assistance was decidedly less than that of comparable families who were not receiving welfare assistance. This comparative immobility of recipients of welfare may very well have been caused by state welfare policies. At that time most states required that residents live in a state for one year before they could receive welfare assistance. It seems likely that these state restrictions limited the interstate mobility of welfare recipients. Welfare-dependent families moved less often across state lines but were more likely than the nonpoor to move within counties and just as likely as the nonpoor to make moves between counties within a state.

Residency requirements were declared unconstitutional by the Supreme Court in 1969, and in the next few years they were eliminated by the states. In the absence of these restrictions the mobility of those receiving welfare increased decidedly, so that by the mid-1970s their long distance mobility was greater than that of nonrecipients (table 1-4). This was the case whether the family consisted of a married couple or was headed by a single woman. The pattern not only held nationwide but was apparent in most regions of the country. Only in the South were recipients less likely to report having moved recently. This southern deviation from the national norm may itself have been welfare-related. It is possible that potential welfare recipients were less likely than nonrecipients to have moved to the South because welfare benefits in that region were lower.

That poor people are more mobile than other Americans should come as no surprise. Blacks participated in a great migration from

25. Between 1968 and 1971 the interstate mobility of poor families with female heads between the ages of 20 and 45 not receiving welfare benefits was greater than the interstate mobility of comparable families not in poverty. Larry Long, *Migration and Residential Mobility in the United States* (Russell Sage, 1988), p. 167.

TABLE 1-3. Families That Made a Long Distance Move,
by Poverty Status, Race, and Region, Selected
Periods, 1975–84[a]
Percent

Poverty status, race, and region[b]	1975–80	1980–81	1983–84
Poor	15.4	6.0	5.4
Nonpoor	14.7	3.7	3.8
Whites			
Poor	16.4	6.9	6.2
Nonpoor	14.8	3.7	3.9
Blacks			
Poor	10.4	2.2	2.6
Nonpoor	10.6	3.1	2.2
Northeast			
Poor	11.6	3.6	3.8
Nonpoor	11.1	2.7	2.8
North central			
Poor	12.7	3.5	4.5
Nonpoor	11.1	2.5	2.7
South			
Poor	13.6	5.9	5.1
Nonpoor	16.4	4.4	4.6
West			
Poor	29.0	11.8	8.7
Nonpoor	21.2	5.4	5.0

Sources: Bureau of the Census, "Geographical Mobility: March 1975 to March 1980," *Current Population Reports*, series P-20, no. 368 (Department of Commerce, 1981), table 35, pp. 96, 101–04, 107, 110–13; "March 1980 to March 1981," no. 377 (1983), table 36, pp. 102–05, 108, 111, 114; and "March 1983 to March 1984," no. 407 (1986), table 36, pp. 108–11, 114, 117, 120.

a. We estimated the number of long distance moves by totaling the number of families that moved between standard metropolitan statistical areas (SMSAs) and non-SMSAs and from one SMSA to another and from abroad. Moves within an SMSA or within rural America were not counted as long distance moves.

b. Poor defined as those living below the poverty line as defined by the Department of Agriculture.

the southern states in search of new economic opportunities during
the two world wars. And apart from politically inspired exoduses,
most international migrations have been conducted by relatively
poor people who had little stake in remaining in the old country.
Labor economists have generally explained this greater mobility of
the poor as a function of the relatively low opportunity costs of
moving for those with low incomes. The contemporary economic

TABLE 1-4. Families That Made a Long Distance Move, by Welfare Status, Type of Household, and Region, Selected Periods, 1975–84[a]

Percent

Welfare status, type of household, and region	1975–80	1980–81	1983–84
Recipient	15.0	5.3	5.6
Nonrecipient	14.7	3.9	3.9
Married couple			
Recipient	18.0	8.0	9.2
Nonrecipient	15.1	4.0	4.0
Female-headed			
Recipient	13.9	4.1	4.1
Nonrecipient	12.3	3.1	3.2
Northeast			
Recipient	11.3	3.5	4.9
Nonrecipient	11.1	2.7	2.7
North central			
Recipient	14.1	3.9	5.3
Nonrecipient	11.0	2.5	2.7
South			
Recipient	10.9	4.2	3.6
Nonrecipient	16.4	4.6	4.7
West			
Recipient	27.9	11.4	9.4
Nonrecipient	21.4	5.6	5.2

Sources: Bureau of the Census, "Geographical Mobility: March 1975 to March 1980," *Current Population Reports*, series P-20, no. 368 (Department of Commerce, 1981), table 35, pp. 96–100; "March 1980 to March 1981," no. 377 (1983), table 35, pp. 97–101; "March 1983 to March 1984," no. 407 (1986), table 35, pp. 103–07.

a. See note a, table 1-3.

circumstances of the poor are so disadvantageous that they encourage exploring alternatives elsewhere.

It is one thing to show that the poor are mobile. It is another to show that welfare benefits influence their choices of where to live. Although the evidence on this point is set forth in later chapters, we wish to clarify from the beginning a point that is often misunderstood. Most of the political debate on welfare-induced migration has focused on immigration—whether poor people come to a state seeking higher benefits. But the cost to a state of high welfare benefits is the same whether the presence of the poor is the result of immigration or of a decision not to emigrate to another state. The real point of concern is net, not gross, migration.

A state with high welfare benefits provides incentives both for the resident poor to remain in the state and for the poor in other states to move there. Even if this second factor is not particularly powerful—that is, even if the immigration of the poor into a state occurs for no other reason than the search for employment or the bringing together of families—the size of the state's low-income population will increase if emigration is not occurring at the same rate. The retention effects of welfare policies may thus be equally or more important in raising the poverty level of the state than the attraction effects. And it is the rising poverty level that causes many state policymakers to become concerned that their policies are a magnet that attracts and retains the poor.

National governments are no less concerned about the magnet effects of their welfare policies. They are well aware that the elaborate welfare programs of prosperous, industrialized nations can attract poor people from foreign countries that have fewer resources and much less adequate welfare systems. But the national government, unlike states, has mechanisms designed to control migration from outside its boundaries. No state can bar a citizen of another state from moving into it and receiving the public services the state makes available to its own citizens. Yet this is precisely what the United States tries to do with illegal immigrants. Although the United States is not always successful in excluding illegal immigrants, it attempts to reduce the magnetic effect of its policies not by cutting its social services but by erecting more effective barriers to entry into the country.

But even though a national government can impose tight immigration restrictions in order to avoid inundation by the poor from other countries, and thus for this reason need not deny its own citizens welfare benefits, there may be other factors that preclude a national government from providing adequate assistance to the poor. In recent years the size of the fiscal deficit and the conservative mood that has pervaded Washington politics seem to have dampened the readiness of the federal government to finance welfare programs.

For these rather practical political reasons some might think it better at the present time to leave welfare policy to state governments. We show in our concluding chapter, however, that these considerations are not as powerful as conventional wisdom might lead one to expect. The poor receiving federally funded SSI benefits (which must meet a nationally determined standard) receive substantially higher benefits than do AFDC recipients, and their benefits have not been reduced during an era of political conservatism and budget constraint.

But if a national benefit would raise welfare levels, is that not reason enough to let states continue to set welfare policy? There are some who believe that higher welfare benefits would weaken family ties and reduce incentives to work.[26] To make this argument is to admit openly that the main reason for state control is to keep benefits low. And it must be conceded that if low benefits are the primary objective, existing governmental arrangements have much to recommend them. But those who favor state control to keep benefits low should recognize that other, perhaps more important, values are adversely affected by a nonuniform state-controlled welfare system. When state benefit programs vary widely, it raises the question: Should government welfare policy influence family decisions about where to live? Most people, we think, would say no. Families should not be motivated to move somewhere or stay where they are living because of differences in welfare benefits. Creating a national standard would enable recipients to move for the same reasons as other people move: to secure better employment, to join a family member, or simply to pursue a brighter future. To the extent that people are choosing a state of residence in order to secure or keep high benefits, government policies are shaping the lives of individuals in ways that most people—conservatives and liberals alike—would find inappropriate.

By removing welfare barriers to residential choice, a national standard would also enhance national economic efficiency. In recent years new employment opportunities have been greater in the South or Southwest, while welfare benefits have been higher in many

26. Charles Murray, *Losing Ground: American Social Policy, 1950–1980* (Basic Books, 1984).

states of the Rust Belt. If benefits are uniform throughout the country, welfare recipients will not be as likely to remain in economically declining areas just because they receive higher benefits there, nor will they be as hesitant to move to more economically promising areas for fear of losing their benefits in the transition. Freeing them from an unnecessary governmental constraint on their choice would not only allow recipients to move to places where their prospects are better but would also improve the economic well-being of the country as a whole.

And what about those who believe that states should have the right to set welfare policy as they wish? Establishing a national standard will, admittedly, restrict the choices available to states. But the present arrangements also restrict state choice, because states that wish to raise their benefits cannot do so without attracting disproportionate numbers of poor people from other parts of the country. And if limiting the choices of states is necessary to expand the choices of individuals, it is probably a trade-off most Americans are willing to make.

The Plan of the Book

Our argument is developed in four steps. Chapter 2 is a case study of welfare policymaking in the state of Wisconsin. In order to provide a context for the more quantitative analysis to follow, we discuss the politics of the welfare magnet and show how it influences the setting of public policy in a particular state. The case study shows how the fear of welfare-induced migration can affect political debate even in a relatively affluent and progressive state; it also shows that the magnet effect is not the only factor affecting state policy. The state's political culture, political competition between the two political parties, and the overall economic climate of the state also shape welfare policy deliberations.

In chapter 3 we draw upon the findings from the case study to identify a set of variables to be used in a quantitative analysis that examines the extent to which the magnet effect is a more general phenomenon in American state politics. Including indicators of the specific factors found to be important in Wisconsin, we identify the determinants of changes in welfare policy for the forty-eight contiguous states and the District of Columbia between 1970 and 1985. The findings from this quantitative analysis indicate that the Wisconsin experience is not exceptional. Changes in welfare policy are influenced by a state's political culture and competitiveness, but are also influenced by the state's poverty rate and by the level of its welfare benefits compared with those in other states.

The quantitative analysis also explores the extent to which the fears of Wisconsin politicians are warranted by looking at the factors that affect changes in poverty rates within a state. We find that a number of economic factors, including a state's wage rates as well as changes in its employment opportunities, are important determinants of state poverty rates. But we also find robust evidence that states with high welfare benefits experience disproportionate growth in their poverty rates.

The fourth chapter describes the processes by which the current system came into being. It identifies the governmental institutions and political forces that have gradually changed a state-controlled welfare system into an intergovernmental system increasingly but still incompletely directed by the federal government. The story of the changing structure of federalism helps identify the forces that have contributed to the centralization of welfare policy as well as the forces that have resisted these changes.

Finally, in chapter 5 we propose a practical step that can go a long way toward achieving a national welfare standard. After setting forth the benefits and costs of this proposal, we assess its political feasibility. Bearing in mind the forces that have shaped national welfare policy in the past, we identify the forces that give us reason to believe a national standard could be adopted in the not too distant future.

Chapter 2

Welfare Politics: A Case Study

T HE BUMPER STICKERS say "Escape to Wisconsin." Meant to lure tourists to enjoy the state's northern woods scenery, the slogan sounded to many people like the advice of Chicago social workers to their welfare clients. In 1985 a three-person family living in Chicago (or anywhere else in Illinois) could receive no more than $520 a month in welfare benefits. If they drove about fifty miles across the border into Kenosha (or anywhere else in Wisconsin) they could get as much as $662 a month. Although escaping to Wisconsin would not make the poor rich—the state's combined AFDC and food stamp benefits left the family's income 6 percent below the poverty line—a short move could increase the family benefits by one-fourth.

Not that many of the poor said they moved across the Wisconsin border just to obtain higher welfare benefits. Instead, they reported to have come for quite respectable reasons that have induced many other Americans to move: "I came to Kenosha because it's closer to visit my family." "I wanted to get my children away from the gangs." "It's hard to find housing in North Chicago." "I thought my children would get a better education." But these explanations do not deny the possibility that welfare benefits played some part in the decision. After all, one recipient noted that her benefits more than doubled after settling in Wisconsin, and that her six sisters—each also receiving welfare—followed her into the state.[1]

1. Quotes of anonymous welfare recipients taken from Dave Backmann, "Family Reasons Draw Recipients," *Kenosha News,* March 18, 1986; and Backmann, "Simple

24

More prosperous Wisconsin residents were not amused. Some were convinced that "all of the trash from Chicago, Waukegan and other places (in Illinois) are dumping themselves on Kenosha" to take advantage of Wisconsin's higher benefits.[2] Much of the anger against welfare recipients was no doubt based on the stereotype that the migrants were shiftless blacks who wanted the state to pay them to take care of their illegitimate children. But there was another reason for taxpayer agitation. It was one thing to help the down-and-out already living in the state. It was another thing entirely, many thought, to help the castoffs from another place. Helping these new arrivals was showing not generosity, but stupidity. Anger was directed not only at the impoverished individuals coming to Wisconsin but also at the system that encouraged them to do so.

It was understandable that the taxpayers of Wisconsin felt abused by the failure of Illinois to take care of its own poverty-stricken. Chicago was accused of giving them "Greyhound therapy": a one-way bus ticket north. Who in Illinois was not better off for this? Greyhound therapy helped Illinois welfare recipients to receive more money, and it also relieved the burden on Illinois taxpayers by reducing their welfare load.

Taxpayer anger was bolstered by official agreement about the source and scope of the welfare problems. Joe Trotta, Kenosha's police chief, complained about the increase in gangs, drugs, and crimes, attributing these problems to welfare migrants. The Kenosha school superintendent worried about the increasing number of migrants in his schools and the growing educational burden they placed on the system. The county supervisor was troubled by the housing problems that welfare migrants created: "We're only six miles from the Illinois border and they're coming every day. Slum landlords are taking advantage of them, and we have blighted

Possessions Justify Her Move," *Kenosha News,* March 17, 1986, in Wisconsin Expenditure Commission, *Report of the Welfare Magnet Study Committee, Appendices* (December 1986), pp. C26–C27, C30–C31. (Hereafter *Welfare Magnet Report, Appendices.*)

2. Letter to the editor signed "Go Back to Illinois," *Kenosha News,* March 16, 1986, in *Welfare Magnet Report, Appendices,* p. C23.

neighborhoods."[3] Kenosha police detective Michael Serpe summed it all up:

> These people [welfare migrants] have no intention of going to work. To believe them when they say they are coming here for jobs is to believe in the tooth fairy. There are no jobs. They are coming here for one reason: Welfare pays more. . . . We seem to have some social thinkers in Madison [the state capital] and a governor who are blind to the problems facing us.[4]

Whether or not Serpe was right about the welfare migrants, he was clearly wrong about the governor. Democratic Governor Anthony Earl was all too conscious of the accusations made against Wisconsin's welfare system. After all, Earl had budget fights coming up in 1985 and a reelection campaign loomed in 1986. Blindness to voters' concerns about welfare could hurt him in both.

The Welfare Magnet Issue

Getting welfare in Wisconsin did not put anyone on Easy Street, but it was not only in comparison with Illinois that Wisconsin seemed generous to its poor. Nationally, in 1985 Wisconsin had the fourth highest AFDC benefits for a family of three. The effect of these welfare policies on the residential choices of poor people became a pervasive theme in the mid-1980s in Wisconsin's welfare policy debates. As we have shown, the issue surfaced in Kenosha, Wisconsin, a town closely adjacent to the Illinois border that seemed to be a particularly attractive locale for many poor people moving to Wisconsin. Although the welfare magnet issue would become a Republican campaign theme in the 1986 gubernatorial election, the Democratic state senator from Kenosha, Joseph Andrea, was one of the first to recognize the political capital inherent in the issue. "Wisconsin is No. 3 in the nation in welfare payments," he observed

3. Arthur L. Srb, "State's Generous Welfare Creating Border-Hopping Problem," *Capital Times*, May 10, 1985, in *Welfare Magnet Report, Appendices*, p. C3.

4. Robert Enstad, "Wisconsin Welfare Bounty a Lure," *Chicago Tribune*, July 14, 1985, in *Welfare Magnet Report, Appendices*, pp. C8–C9.

in the summer of 1985, "and we're shooting for second place and the silver medal in the welfare olympics."[5] Saying that the streets of Kenosha were lined with cars bearing Illinois license plates, Andrea claimed, "I've seen them, and they're not here for a social visit." Though he was willing to cite some statistics about Kenosha's welfare caseload, he admitted that his evidence was based primarily on personal observation. He rejected the need for further analysis: "I don't think we have to have another survey to tell me something I already know."[6]

The focus of Andrea's complaints was Democratic Governor Earl's proposal to increase welfare benefits by a modest 3 percent, an amount that did not even keep pace with increases in the cost of living. His criticisms were quickly picked up by the state's Republican opposition. Representative David Prosser noted that Wisconsin's appellation as the "dairy state" might need to be changed to the "welfare state."[7] Prosser, along with another Republican representative, Betty Jo Nelson, argued that Wisconsin already offered higher benefits than almost any other state in the country and that raising its benefits further would severely strain the state's tax capacity.

Governor Earl had anticipated these criticisms of his proposed increase in welfare benefits by asking the state's Department of Health and Social Services (DHSS) to commission a study to find out the effect of Wisconsin's welfare policies on migration. The commission, chaired by John Torphy, the deputy secretary of the DHSS, reached ambiguous conclusions in its study, completed in early May 1985. Using 1980 census data, it reported that on the one hand Wisconsin had gained 4,600 people with below poverty-level incomes and 1,880 welfare recipients between 1975 and 1980. On the other hand, people with higher incomes had moved into the

5. Enstad, "Wisconsin Welfare Bounty a Lure," p. C8. Exactly where Wisconsin ranked depended on the precise definition of benefit levels one used. Senator Andrea seems to have picked the definition that best suited his political purpose.

6. Cliff Miller, "How Strong Is the 'Welfare Magnet'?" *Isthmus,* May 31, 1985; and Bill Novak, "Senator Andrea Says . . . Welfare Survey Unnecessary," *Sheboygan Press,* July 5, 1986, in *Welfare Magnet Report, Appendices,* pp. C7, C42.

7. Thomas W. Still, "Dems Defeat Attempts to Cap Welfare Program," *Wisconsin State Journal,* May 10, 1985, in *Welfare Magnet Report, Appendices,* p. C4.

state at about the same rate and from about the same places as
welfare recipients, so it could appear that the poor moved in for
about the same reasons as anyone else. Torphy said that the report
was not definitive because "census data on migration does not . . .
ask why people migrated."[8] Without this data, Torphy believed, it
was impossible to show conclusively how much welfare affected the
steady stream of poor moving in.

The welfare magnet issue thus continued to simmer. After the
Democrats pushed the 3 percent welfare increase through the state
legislature, those concerned about the magnet effect turned their
attention to limiting the availability of these increased benefits to
new residents. Early in the fall of 1985 Republican State Senator
Michael Ellis produced some back-of-the-envelope numbers showing
that over 35 percent of Wisconsin's AFDC caseload had migrated
in from Illinois and other states. Ellis (overlooking the Supreme
Court decision that forbade restrictions on welfare availability to
new residents) called for residency requirements. The Milwaukee
Social Services Committee also voted for legislation mandating a
six-month requirement.[9] Legislation restricting the ability of newcomers to receive welfare was in fact enacted, but it applied not to
AFDC but only to general relief, which was entirely funded by the
state. Although perhaps symbolically satisfying, the legislation was
filled with loopholes. It stipulated that no migrants could receive
benefits for sixty days unless they were born in Wisconsin, had
previously lived there for at least a year, had come to the state to
join a relative during a medical emergency, were suffering unusual
hardship, or had not come to Wisconsin for the purpose of applying
for welfare. With the inclusion of this last proviso, the legislation
lost its teeth, because aid could be denied only to those who admitted
that they moved into the state to collect welfare. As of August 1986,
only 1 of the 13,000 new applicants for welfare in the southernmost
six counties of the state had been denied on the basis of this law.[10]

8. Miller, "How Strong Is the 'Welfare Magnet'?"
9. Editorial by State Representative Marcia P. Coggs, "Data Dispel Idea that
State Is Welfare Haven," *Milwaukee Journal*, September 24, 1985, in *Welfare Magnet
Report, Appendices*, p. C11.
10. Scott Hildebrand, "Few Denied Welfare Aid," *Green Bay Press-Gazette*,

Whatever symbolic effect the legislation might have had was short lasting, however, for the welfare magnet issue did not disappear. The immediate cause of its revival was the unconstitutional budget deficit the state began to run in early 1986. The economy had not improved as much as Governor Earl had hoped, so government revenues were running behind the previous year's projections. In order to bring the budget into balance, Earl and the legislature had to start looking for places to cut $53 million, and welfare was one obvious place.

The timing of the projected budget deficit aggravated the issue. This was an election year, and a governor who was too generous with welfare recipients, too careless with the state's budget, and too negligent of the state's economy could be in big trouble in the fall. Governor Earl was aware of the strong sentiment in southern Wisconsin against welfare migrants and, despite the lack of evidence supporting the welfare magnet concept in the DHSS's study, admitted that such migration had been "a problem" for half a decade and had increased in the last few years.[11] To help placate the voters, Earl had his appointees at DHHS start developing plans for a Welfare Magnet Commission to undertake a new and larger study. It was also hoped that the new study would develop more definitive data about people's reasons for migrating.

The announcement of the study did not succeed in removing the issue even temporarily from the political agenda, however. As Senator Andrea observed,

Virtually everyone today concedes that to some degree our national third-place level of AFDC benefits have a role in attracting in-migrants to Wisconsin from Illinois and other states. What bothers me is . . . that this issue must be studied to death before we actually do anything about the problem.[12]

September 23, 1986; and "Toothless Law," *Beloit Daily News*, September 23, 1986, in *Welfare Magnet Report, Appendices*, p. C53.

11. Rick Romell, "Kenosha's Welfare Immigrants Causing Some Serious Concern," *Milwaukee Sentinel*, January 24, 1986, in *Welfare Magnet Report, Appendices*, pp. C14–C15.

12. Editorial by Matt Pommer, "Let's Take a Closer Look," *Watertown Daily Times*, April 28, 1986, in *Welfare Magnet Report, Appendices*, p. C34.

Mark Rogacki, the executive director of the Wisconsin Counties Association, stated much the same opinion:

> Quite frankly, we find ourselves asking why we must continually devote more of Wisconsin's limited financial resources to proving that the problems we already know exist, actually do. Instead of commissioning another study, the commission would be better advised to focus its attention on recommended solutions to the AFDC/welfare problems of Wisconsin.
>
> . . . We cannot justify the expenditure of limited taxpayer resources to confirm what we already know to be true—Wisconsin is a welfare magnet.[13]

Clearly, no study—especially one that was less than definitive—was going to settle the political aspects of the welfare magnet issue. Because Governor Earl had originally proposed the increased funding for welfare, any panel he appointed would face suspicion if it found that benefit levels did not affect migration. And any study conducted under DHSS auspices that found no magnet effects would be met with the usual skepticism toward self-aggrandizing bureaucracies. As one writer summed it up, "It seems that just about everyone except some Ivory Tower professors and state bureaucrats is convinced that people are being lured here by higher benefits."[14]

Rebutting his critics, Earl called for a bipartisan approach to solving the problems of poverty and urged Wisconsin's citizens "to put aside the most insidious doctrine of all—that people are on welfare because they like it." He also rejected the idea that Wisconsin was a welfare magnet, arguing that the poor left Illinois to escape the gangs and the ghettos; furthermore, he noted, both Minnesota and Michigan offered higher welfare benefits than did Wisconsin.

---

13. Matt Pommer, "State Anti-Welfare Zealots Should Demagnetize Anti-Family Stance," *Capitol Times,* April 28, 1986, in *Welfare Magnet Report, Appendices,* p. C35.

14. Rogacki pointed out that the head of the study commission was Bernard Stumbras, who was on leave from his administrative job at DHSS, which in the past had backed welfare increases. Norm Monson, "We Are 'Welfare Magnet'; How Can Anyone Doubt It?" *Racine Shoreline Leader,* July 31, 1986, in *Welfare Magnet Report, Appendices,* pp. C46–C47.

(They did not, though they were close.) He reminded people that Wisconsin was a humane state that traditionally had not neglected its poor. Rather than relying on outdated Great Society programs, however, it should use another of its traditions—its creativity—to design a welfare system that truly helped the poor.[15] The governor's position was backed by Michael Soika, a spokesman for the Roman Catholic archdiocese of Milwaukee, who challenged the notion that AFDC recipients were living high on the hog. "At the very time we have more poor people, we have a national debate on how much poorer we can make them."[16]

Detecting little enthusiasm for the governor's position, Senator Andrea claimed that "I was one of the only ones to label Wisconsin a welfare haven at the start. But as the months went by, the legislators from the border districts agreed that I was right."[17] One of these legislators, the Democratic state senator from Racine, a border town not far from Kenosha, developed his own proposal to "demagnetize" Wisconsin's welfare benefits. He proposed that Wisconsin simply pay any welfare recipients what they had been paid before they moved into the state. A prominent Republican state representative who served on the powerful Joint Finance Committee, when asked whether this was simply an attempt by the Democrats to steal a politically potent campaign issue, replied "No. I think's it's politically smart of them because there's a train coming and it would be stupid for them to stand in the middle of the tracks."[18] But Republican Finance Committee members and border-area Democrats were not the worst of Governor Earl's worries. The Republicans chose the state Assembly minority leader, Tommy Thompson, a consistent critic of excessive social spending, to be their standard-bearer in the 1986 election.

In the subsequent campaign, Thompson portrayed increased

---

15. Tom Murphy, "Governor Calls for New Ways to Break Welfare Dependency," *Green Bay Press-Gazette,* June 26, 1986; and Art Srb, "Even Dems Talking of Welfare Reform," *Oshkosh Northwestern,* August 3, 1986, in *Welfare Magnet Report, Appendices,* pp. C40, C48.

16. "Opinions Differ on Welfare Funding," *Portage Daily Register,* August 19, 1986, in *Welfare Magnet Report, Appendices,* p. C51.

17. Novak, "Senator Andrea Says . . . Welfare Survey Unnecessary."

18. Srb, "Even Dems Talking of Welfare Reform."

welfare spending as one of many ill-advised attempts at throwing money at problems that state governments cannot solve. Even Earl began to voice doubts about his own welfare policies. He went so far as to draw conclusions not much different from those Senator Andrea had drawn more than a year before: "If I were a mother in Cabrini Green [the notoriously bad housing project in Chicago], . . . I would consider getting a bicycle and cart and moving" up to Wisconsin.[19] Earl's conversion came too late, however. Thompson's attacks on Earl's overspending, excessive taxes, welfare, and the location of a state prison were enough.[20] He decisively defeated Earl with a strong 53–47 percent margin. Yet no one expected the welfare issue to be an easy one for the new governor. Even on the morning after the election, the newspapers were predicting that the likely fight between Thompson and the legislature would be over his desire to cut AFDC benefits.[21]

The Economy and Business Climate

As potent a single issue as the welfare magnet question had become, it was probably most significant as a chord in a larger political theme that had become an all-consuming concern in this midwestern state: the threats to the Wisconsin economy posed by national and international competition. The budget bill in which Governor Earl's welfare increase was embedded was bitterly assailed by his future Republican opponent as too high on spending and too low on creating growth. Other Republicans suggested that the workers at the endangered Oscar Mayer meat-packing firm in Madison should be asked if they wanted to pay for higher welfare benefits. Democrats replied that inasmuch as many employees were being laid off, they might well need AFDC once their unemployment benefits expired.

Economic decline was an especially painful topic in Wisconsin

19. "Are Welfare Seekers Escaping to Wisconsin?" *Stevens Point Journal*, August 19, 1986, in *Welfare Magnet Report, Appendices*, p. C51.

20. Doug Mell, "It'll Be Governor Thompson," *Wisconsin State Journal*, November 5, 1986.

21. Doug Mell, "Thompson's Ideas Will Clash with Legislature," *Wisconsin State Journal*, November 5, 1986.

politics, because the state had historically been a "cheese and beer" state that enjoyed a varied economy producing always-needed staples. Never a wealthy state—its average income did not reach the national average until 1979—it nonetheless had a diversified economy with, roughly speaking, a third of its wages and salaries coming from manufacturing, a third from government and service employment, and a third spread out among such sectors as agriculture, construction, transportation, sales, and finance.[22] This balance had generally kept Wisconsin's economy on a fairly even keel, but cracks began to appear in the 1980s when both the manufacturing and agricultural sectors suffered sharp setbacks. The average income dropped a few points below the national norm and remained below that of two of its immediate neighbors, Illinois and Minnesota.

The manufacturing sector was particularly in trouble. At the low point of the 1982 recession, manufacturing employment had dropped more than 20 percent from its high point in 1979; by 1985 it had recovered only about a quarter of this loss.[23] Visible employers such as American Motors and Oscar Mayer had laid off large numbers of employees and were threatening to close down entirely. Employment in automobile manufacturing had fallen by more than 30 percent. Few thought that Wisconsin was going bankrupt, but many were concerned that it was losing out to other states in its ability to maintain and create jobs, businesses, and economic growth.[24]

Although it was obvious that the economic problems Wisconsin faced were also widespread throughout the country during the recession, Wisconsinites did not blame outside forces entirely for their economic troubles. Wisconsin's citizens (for reasons discussed below) are likely to see problems as having causes and solutions within their control. As a result, the issue crystallized into a debate over Wisconsin's "business climate."

22. Mark Rom, "The Political Economy of the Midwest," in Peter K. Eisinger and William Gormley, eds., *The Midwest Response to the New Federalism* (University of Wisconsin Press, 1988), p. 21.

23. Rom, "Political Economy of the Midwest," p. 25.

24. Even the federal trough had been closed down, with Wisconsin ranking forty-seventh among states in the per capita outlays it received from Washington for defense (the only category of federal outlays growing substantially); overall, per capita federal outlays to Wisconsin were only 75 percent of the national average. Rom, "Political Economy of the Midwest," p. 29.

A business climate, scholars say, is the "non-physical environment for enterprise," the political and social factors that are thought to influence business decisions about where to locate or expand.[25] Like the "natural climate" (averages and fluctuations in such things as temperature, rainfall, and sunlight), the business climate is a complex concept comprising a wide variety of factors involving quality of life, labor characteristics, and government policy. Higher taxes, more extensive social welfare systems, and more generous worker benefits are counted as hurting the business climate. Government-provided services such as education, parks, hospitals, and public safety improve it. Groups conducting business climate studies typically rank each state based on its average score on these variables, with the lowest-ranked states having the worst climate. From the 1960s to the early 1980s, there was some evidence that businesses were moving to, or expanding employment in, the states with good business climates, while reducing their activity in the ones with poor climates.[26] Although the rankings from the different studies vary slightly, Wisconsin sat toward the bottom of most lists and one prominent study rated it thirty-ninth of the forty-eight contiguous states.[27]

Although scholarly studies may show that the business climate can affect firms' location choices, the issue can become considerably

25. See James S. Fisher and Dean M. Hanink, "Business Climate: Behind the Geographic Shift of American Manufacturing," *Economic Review,* Federal Reserve Bank of Atlanta, vol. 67 (June 1982), pp. 20–31. The best-known ratings of the business climates of the states are the Fantus Company, *Comparative Business Climate Study* (Chicago: Illinois Manufacturers Association, 1975) (the Fantus study); and Alexander Grant and Company, *A Study of Business Climate of the Forty-Eight Contiguous States of America* (Chicago: Conference of State Manufacturer's Associations, 1979) (the Grant study). The Grant study has been done yearly since 1979; today it is formally called the "Manufacturing Climates Study" and is done by the accounting firm of Grant Thornton. See James Litke, "New Hampshire, S. Dakota Are Tops in Business Survey," *Washington Post,* July 14, 1988, p. F2. The Grant study includes business expenses such as labor costs in its rankings; Fisher and Hanink do not.

26. Fisher and Hanink, "Business Climate," pp. 23–30; John S. Hekman, "What Are Businesses Looking For?" *Economic Review,* Federal Reserve Bank of Atlanta, vol. 67 (June 1982), pp. 6–19; and Roger W. Schmenner, *Making Business Location Decisions* (Prentice-Hall, 1982).

27. Fisher and Hanink, "Business Climate," pp. 23–30. This was for 1967–75.

more complicated in state politics, mainly because these effects are hard to detect and open to dispute. For one thing, business climate has less effect on location decisions than do conventional factors such as proximity to markets and overall production costs.[28] Second, even if companies see other places as having a better business climate, most companies do not move to another state to take advantage of it (although *threatening* to do so could extract concessions from the home state's government). Third, while taxes and welfare spending are thought to hurt a state's climate, spending policies contributing to higher quality of life (more education, parks, and hospitals) improve it. Of course, businesses prefer to pay lower taxes, but since spending is impossible without taxes it is an open question whether they are willing to sacrifice the gains in quality of life that some types of public spending can produce.

Wisconsin politicians were nonetheless very sensitive to charges that they were doing anything to hurt the business climate and were anxious to demonstrate that they were indeed improving it. Wisconsin's economy was undergoing some wrenching adjustments, and firms apparently were taking jobs south to states with more favorable business climates. Other states—especially those in the Sun Belt—emphasized their superior business climates in advertisements designed to lure business. Once these states started promoting their favorable climates, it was easy for states with lower rankings (such as Wisconsin) to become nervous about losing jobs unless they took steps to meet the competition. This nervousness increased when job layoffs occurred and businesses threatened to move.

Welfare policy accordingly became more contentious as Wisconsin's economy became shakier, its business climate more salient, and its benefit levels increasingly different from those of its neighbors. In debate over what the appropriate benefit levels should be, almost never did one hear moral questions concerning, for example, whether the poor "deserve" welfare. Instead, the issues revolved around the consequences for Wisconsin's economic position. Would raising benefits bring in additional recipients? Would it raise demand for other welfare-related services as well?

28. Schmenner, *Making Business Location Decisions.*

The debate over business climate was also the central theme of state gubernatorial politics. The gubernatorial race in 1982, for example, had pitted candidates with sharply differing views about what created the conditions conducive to prosperity. Republican businessman Terry Kohler had campaigned on a platform of cutting taxes and reducing government's role in the economy. Democrat Anthony Earl, who had worked in state government virtually all his adult life, had explicitly advocated active government and greater taxes to provide education, public transportation, and other social services, claiming that the increased tax burden would be outweighed in businesses' eyes by the extra services and amenities government provided.[29] In the voters' eyes, apparently, Earl was right—at least in 1982—as he soundly beat Kohler by a 57–43 margin.

Earl's good fortune continued into 1985; indeed, his 1985–87 budget was, in many ways, a politician's dream.[30] High economic growth in 1985, which had increased tax revenues faster than had been anticipated, allowed the governor both to cut taxes (on average, income taxes were cut by 8 percent) and to raise spending (by just under 6 percent each year).[31] The 3 percent welfare increases that caused so much controversy were embedded in a budget composed in this period of high optimism. Yet it can hardly be said that Earl threw his business sense to the winds. The greater welfare spending did not keep pace with increases in the cost of living and accounted for a only a small portion of the growth in expenditures. Also, benefit increases were less than increases given to others. While AFDC benefits grew by 3 percent, all state employees received pay raises of 6 percent. Faculty members at the University of Wisconsin-Madison gained 15 percent.[32]

29. Rom, "Political Economy of the Midwest," p. 41.

30. At that time Wisconsin had biennial, rather than yearly, budgets. It has since switched to annual budgets, in part because of the difficulty in accurately predicting revenues and expenditures in the second year of the cycle.

31. Because of biennial budgeting, it was often difficult to interpret how much spending and taxes actually were changing on an annual basis; although the two-year budget increased by 18 percent over the previous two-year plan, it is not possible to tell how much of this increase was in any one year.

32. "Legislature OK's '85–87 Budget," *Wisconsin State Journal,* June 30, 1985.

Nor was welfare provision the policy least sensitive to the concerns of Wisconsin's business community. A major plank in Governor Earl's policy platform was a very contentious comparable worth program intended to redress the pay differentials between women and men working for the state. The $9.1 million allotted to this program was debated much more heatedly than virtually any other issue. Although comparable worth was divisive for a number of reasons, one of the main objections raised was the ill effect some thought it would have on the state's business climate. Opponents feared that comparable worth, by raising the wages of women working for the government, would also drive wages up in Wisconsin's private sector; they also worried that once comparable worth was implemented for the government, the inevitable next step was to impose it on private businesses. For those who thought a state's business climate depended on lower wages and little government economic intervention, both prospects were troubling. In the end the Democratically controlled legislature accepted half the governor's proposal, taking the safe course of buying both halves of the argument.

Although Earl's comparable worth proposal disturbed business leaders, the governor did not always ignore their expressed concerns. In 1984 he vetoed a $61 million appropriation for increases in unemployment compensation that the legislature had passed against the nearly universal opposition of the state's business community.[33] Even so, the citizens seemed less sure in 1986 than in 1982 that Earl was correct about the way to build up the state's economy. In his reelection bid Governor Earl faced an outspoken critic of his policies who consistently argued that Wisconsin needed to improve its business climate. Like the previous Republican gubernatorial candidate, Tommy Thompson thought that the best way to do that was to cut taxes, social spending, and environmental and workplace regulations.

The Republican campaign won considerable favor in the business

---

33. Rom, "Political Economy of the Midwest," p. 41. During the 1986 electoral campaign, some observers speculated that Earl's core liberal constituency was prepared to desert him because he had made so many policy concessions to business interests.

community. Just before the election, an independent business group (Businessmen of Wisconsin—Words of Warning, or BOW-WOW) ran an advertisement in the *Wall Street Journal* proclaiming "Escape *FROM* Wisconsin."[34] This ad, which did not mention the ongoing gubernatorial campaign or endorse either candidate, was highly critical of what it saw as the jackboot of Wisconsin's government (and organized labor) on businesses' collective necks. It warned businesses not to come there and excused the ones that found fit to leave.[35] While a number of businesses were highly critical of BOW-WOW (calling their negative campaign foolish and counterproductive) and responded with their own set of national advertisements describing Wisconsin's business virtues, BOW-WOW did help keep the business climate issue solidly in the political debate.

In this debate, the connection between Wisconsin's business climate and welfare policy was made quite explicitly by Wisconsin politicians. The issue was not simply the fact that Wisconsin's welfare policy was attracting poor people to the state. Instead, it was part of a larger debate over the kinds of public policies the state needed to pursue to enhance its economic prosperity. When Governor Earl, defending his increase in AFDC funding the previous year, chastised his Republican opponent for wanting to hurt the poor, Thompson replied, "I'm sorry you can't understand basic econ 101."[36] In his view, any basic economics course would reveal how high taxes, high spending, a policy of comparable worth, and generous welfare policies contributed to a state's economic problems. The view seems to have been widely shared. Thompson, merely by saying "no" to Earl's unpopular programs, came to be seen as offering the better chance of prosperity.

A Moralistic Political Culture

If concerns about the Wisconsin economy helped shape the welfare debate, so did the "political culture" of the state. The term is elusive,

34. Wendy L. Wall, "Changing a Preposition Sure Gets Lots of People Riled in Wisconsin," *Wall Street Journal*, November 3, 1986, p. 35.

35. *Wisconsin State Journal*, October 24, 1986.

36. "Thompson, Earl Spar," *Wisconsin State Journal*, October 24, 1986.

and the way in which it affects public policy can be hard to describe, but there seem to be policy consequences of what Daniel Elazar has called "the particular pattern of orientation to political action in which each political system is embedded."[37] This orientation

> may be found among politicians and the general public, and it may affect their understanding of what politics is and what can be expected from government, influence the types of people who become active in politics, and influence the ways in which they practice politics and formulate public policy.[38]

Elazar distinguishes among three cultural types. In moralistic cultures, the one of greatest relevance here, "both the general public and the politicians conceive of politics as a public activity centered on some notion of the public good and properly devoted to the advancement of the public interest."[39] Political parties are groups intent on obtaining policy goals; they compete over issues, and the party is subordinate to principles. Parties try to win elections not just to gain power but to implement programs.

Moralistic political cultures may have a liberal tint, but they should not be mistaken as synonymous with liberal political parties; conservative parties in moralistic cultures also believe that their policies are beneficial to the public good.[40] In Wisconsin, which has one of the most moralistic political cultures,[41] the Democratic and Republican parties simply have different interpretations of how best

37. Daniel J. Elazar, *American Federalism: A View from the States,* 2d ed. (Thomas Crowell, 1972), pp. 84–85.

38. Ira Sharkansky, "The Utility of Elazar's Political Culture: A Research Note," *Polity,* vol. 2 (Fall 1969), p. 67.

39. Daniel J. Elazar, "The States and the Political Setting," in Ira Sharkansky, ed., *Policy Analysis in Political Science* (Chicago: Markham Publishing Co., 1970), pp. 171–85, quote on p. 174.

40. This is in sharp contrast with parties in what Elazar calls traditionalist or individualist states, where liberal or conservative labels can serve as masks for those simply seeking personal enrichment. See Elazar, *American Federalism.*

41. Sharkansky created a scale to measure the culture of individual states. On a scale of 0 (most moralist) to 9 (most traditional), Minnesota (1.0) was ranked most moralist, with Wisconsin (2.0) in a tie for third with several other states. Sharkansky, "Utility of Elazar's Political Culture," pp. 66–83.

to serve such public needs as creating a prosperous economy and serving the poor. Both parties support government spending to promote the public interest, though they may differ as to the particular uses to which this money should be put. The willingness of Wisconsin's citizens and policymakers to devote resources to public services can be clearly seen in the state's tax effort.[42] Wisconsin's tax effort has consistently been well above the national average; by 1985 it was 37 percent above the country's norms. Although Wisconsin's pockets (as measured by its per capita income) are not deeper than other states', it is more willing to dig deeply in them to find funds for the programs it supports, including programs for the disadvantaged. In 1941 Wisconsin was in the top third among the states in providing welfare, old age assistance, and aid to the blind; by 1961 it had climbed into the top ten in each category.[43]

The origins of Wisconsin's moralistic political culture are in part ethnic, but these ethnic features have evolved during the twentieth century to create two issue-oriented political parties. Wisconsin strongly supported the North in the Civil War, and migration patterns brought literate, liberal, Lutheran Scandinavians "who affiliated themselves with the anti-slavery, anti-liquor, anti-Catholic Yankees in the Republican party."[44] The Germans and the Slavs who came later tended to become Democrats. In the first decades of the 1900s, the Democratic party was weak, while the dominant Republican party was split between the conservative wing and the liberal followers of Robert La Follette. These factions were formalized during the 1930s when La Follette's followers split off to form the Progressive party, which competed with the Republicans in statewide elections. After the Progressive party was disbanded (and

42. The tax effort is the ratio of a state's actual tax collections to its tax capacity, while tax capacity is the amount of revenue each state would raise if it applied a national average set of tax rates for twenty-six commonly used tax bases. Advisory Commission on Intergovernmental Relations, *Significant Features of Fiscal Federalism, 1984 Edition* (ACIR, 1985), pp. 131–32.

43. Herbert Jacob and Kenneth N. Vines, eds., *Politics in the American States: A Comparative Analysis* (Little, Brown, 1965), pp. 390–91.

44. John H. Fenton, *Midwest Politics* (Holt, Rinehart and Winston, 1966), p. 76. Though Fenton was referring directly to Minnesota in this quote, it applies as well to Wisconsin.

Robert La Follette, Jr., beaten by Joseph McCarthy in the 1946 senatorial election), many disgruntled Wisconsin Progressives joined the urban immigrants in a liberal Democratic party. The merging of the Progressives, immigrants, farmers, and laborers brought together those groups that demanded a more egalitarian distribution of goods and opportunities. Those remaining in the Wisconsin Republican party—the Yankee, non-Scandinavian, Protestant conservatives—supported the existing division of goods and opportunities and sought to minimize the intervention of the government into economic affairs.[45]

The Progressive party also reflected the moralistic culture in its commitment to solving social problems through investigation and experimentation. One aspect of this was the "Wisconsin idea," in which the universities were considered not merely ivory towers of abstract reasoning but instead were asked to try to solve the practical issues facing the state and its citizens.[46] Another was the view that the state government should be highly professional, with expert, neutral agencies and an adequately staffed legislature.[47] Wisconsin's political culture suggested that important issues should be settled not by power and prejudice but by reasoned analysis.

45. See Fenton, *Midwest Politics* ; and Daniel J. Elazar, *Cities of the Prairie: The Metropolitan Frontier and American Politics* (Basic Books, 1970).

46. For example, because of the importance of dairies to Wisconsin's economy, the agricultural economics and animal husbandry departments at the University of Wisconsin were leaders in practical dairy research, and the university's extension service actively disseminated the results to dairies throughout the state. Brigitta Young, "The Dairy Sector: From Atomistic Market Structure to a Complex Web of Institutional Arrangements," paper prepared for the 1986 annual meeting of the American Political Science Association.

47. Wisconsin's legislature has one of the oldest and most highly respected research libraries (the Legislative Reference Bureau) and "policy shops" (the Legislative Fiscal Bureau) in the country. Overall, Wisconsin's legislature has been rated very highly (in terms of being "functional, accountable, informed, independent and representative") compared with that of other states. The Citizens Conference on State Legislatures, *State Legislatures: An Evaluation of Their Effectiveness* (Praeger, 1971). See also Ronald D. Hedlund and Patricia K. Freeman, "A Strategy for Measuring the Performance of Legislatures in Processing Decisions," *Legislative Studies Quarterly*, vol. 6 (February 1981), pp. 87–113; and Ronald D. Hedlund and Keith E. Hamm, "Institutional Innovation and Performance Effectiveness in Public Policy Making," in Leroy N. Rieselbach, ed., *Legislative Reform: The Policy Impact* (D.C. Heath, 1978), pp. 117–32.

When Governor Earl was criticized for raising welfare benefits to a level that attracted migrants from other states, it was therefore only natural that he should attempt to address this issue by asking the state's Department of Health and Social Services to study the question. If some state politicians thought the answer was obvious, most politicians probably felt the matter was worth serious examination.

The moralistic culture was particularly evident when the governor commissioned a second study after the first commission, using only census data, reached inconclusive results. Accepting the argument that interview data were necessary to find the reasons poor people moved to Wisconsin, the governor appointed a welfare magnet commission and gave it the funds to interview a large number of welfare recipients. Admittedly, the governor may have used the commission device to deflect criticism during a particularly competitive political campaign. The commission decided that its work was so extensive it could not produce a report until after the November elections, a timing decision that may or may not have been in Governor Earl's political interests. On the one hand, he was attacked for merely studying a problem that others thought needed to be addressed immediately. On the other hand, he could avoid doing anything about the problem—such as cutting welfare benefits—for as long as the topic was being studied.

When the commission did report, it produced a set of findings that are worth discussing at some length—both for what they reveal about welfare policy and for what they suggest about the political implications of such studies. The study relied on interviews with welfare applicants and data on AFDC applicant characteristics from the DHSS files. The primary conclusion from both was inconclusive: "From the several and diverse pieces of information consulted in this study, a common conclusion emerged that the 'welfare magnet' argument *is not without support*. . . . But, given the limitations of these data, competing explanations for the observed patterns can be articulated."[48]

Because the issue had been framed as a question of whether or

48. Wisconsin Expenditure Commission, *Report of the Welfare Magnet Study Committee,* p. iv (emphasis added).

not Wisconsin attracted welfare migrants, the study looked only at one-half of the migration flow—the numbers and characteristics of those moving to Wisconsin. It ignored the possibility that welfare benefits discouraged poor Wisconsinites from moving elsewhere. Still, it found some evidence that a welfare magnet existed. Of the AFDC applicants who had moved into the state in the previous five years, about 10 percent mentioned that welfare benefits played "some role" in their decision; about 30 percent of those applying for benefits very quickly after moving in may have been so influenced. But because most recipients were either Wisconsin natives or had previously lived there, only a very small number—"roughly 3 percent"—of applicants were migrants for whom welfare affected their decisions to move to Wisconsin. For the vast majority of migrants, the most important factor was to be closer to family members.

Even though the effect of welfare benefits on in-migration appeared to be small, the study recognized that "local problems . . . can emerge with considerable force in given communities" because migrants tended to settle in a few areas. These problems could be especially difficult "if the newcomers represent shifts in the character of the local caseload, in the race and ethnic composition of established neighborhoods, and in the populations served by specialized community services."[49] In other words, the problem was not merely that "welfare migrants" cost the state more in AFDC benefits, but also that they created much broader social and political problems. The study concluded on a note quite characteristic of the moralistic tradition in Wisconsin's politics:

Because of the very important contributions of family ties and quality of life considerations in the motivational make-up of migrant AFDC applicants in the state, it would appear that very deep cuts indeed would have to be made to current AFDC program benefits before any impact on the migration of low income persons to the state could be observed. And the brunt of these cuts in

49. Wisconsin Expenditure Commission, *Report of the Welfare Magnet Study Committee*, p. v.

welfare assistance would be borne by families the majority of whom have never lived outside Wisconsin.[50]

A Competitive Political System

It is not enough to say that Wisconsin's political culture produces parties that stand for clearly defined and distinct positions; this distinction would not matter if one party completely dominated the other. Party differences do matter in Wisconsin because the competition is so vigorous and so close. Even though Democrats have had a majority in the state legislature for most of the past few decades, the margin is rarely large enough for them to take this status for granted. The governorship also swings regularly between the parties, with Democrats winning it in six of the eleven elections before 1988. Although the party organizations themselves are not strong (in the sense of being hierarchical political machines providing tangible rewards to their followers), large numbers of citizens (in comparison with those in other states) turn out to vote for their party's candidates during elections.

Within Wisconsin's Assembly and Senate the political competition between the parties is also intense and institutionalized: partisan lines are clearly drawn and usually followed.[51] Budget politics within the legislature illustrate well the pattern of partisan conflict. It is a three-act play in which all the players know their roles. First, the Joint Finance Committee considers the governor's budget proposals.[52] The majority in the legislature dominates this committee,

50. Wisconsin Expenditure Commission, *Report of the Welfare Magnet Study Committee,* p. v.

51. The partisan Assembly and Senate campaign committees are also more important in Wisconsin than in most other states. See Andrew Aoki and Mark Rom, "How Big the PIG? Campaign Contributions, Legislative Vote Scores, and Wisconsin's Party-in-Government," paper prepared for the 1987 annual meeting of the Northeast Political Science Association.

52. The Joint Finance Committee is especially powerful, with jurisdiction over both revenues and appropriations combined in one joint Senate-Assembly committee. For a discussion of this committee's broad functions, see Mark C. Rom and John F. Witte, "Power versus Participation: The Wisconsin State Budget Process," in Sheldon F. Danziger and John F. Witte, eds., *State Policy Choices: The Wisconsin Experience* (University of Wisconsin Press, 1988), pp. 13–34.

and virtually all committee votes proceed strictly along partisan lines. After the committee approves the bill, it goes first to one legislative house and then to the other. Within each house, the majority party caucus is dominant. Within each caucus, the budget is modified until it is sure to have enough votes to pass on the floor; members of the majority party are the only ones who can really make changes. Finally, the Assembly and Senate pass the bill submitted by their majority caucuses. The minority party attempts to amend it on the floor; the majority party beats back each amendment. On the important votes on the floor, partisan lines are again followed. At each stage (Joint Finance Committee, majority party caucus, floor), the majority party almost entirely controls the process. But unlike the dominant party in a one-party state, it does so warily, for it knows that its decisions can be used to drive it from office by the other party.

Conflict between the legislature and the governor is also institutionalized, becoming especially obvious when each is controlled by a different party. The legislature is by national standards well paid, well staffed, and well educated: it resembles a "mini-Congress."[53] It is not dominated by the governor. However, governors are not without resources of their own. Although the office does not rank at the top of the states in terms of formal powers, the governor does develop the budget for the legislature's consideration and exercise line-item vetoes over the legislature's decisions.[54] The budget approved by the legislature contains the vast majority of the governor's proposals.[55]

The intensity of party competition was everywhere evident in the debate over welfare policy. When Republicans in 1985 pictured increased welfare assistance as harmful to the state's economy, Democrats attempted to refute their arguments. For example,

53. Neal R. Peirce and Jerry Hagstrom, *The Book of America: Inside 50 States Today,* rev. ed. (Warner Books, 1983), pp. 272–73.
54. See Thad L. Beyle, "Governors," in Virginia Gray, Herbert Jacob, and Kenneth N. Vines, eds., *Politics in the American States : A Comparative Analysis,* 4th ed. (Little, Brown, 1983); and Alan Rosenthal, *Legislative Life: People, Process, and Performance in the States* (Harper and Row, 1981), p. 237.
55. James Gosling, "The Wisconsin Budgetary Process: A Study of Participant Influence and Choice," Ph.D. dissertation, University of Wisconsin, 1980.

Democratic Representative Travis Davis, from a liberal legislative district near the state capitol, criticized a Republican attempt to freeze assistance at current levels as a "most distasteful [proposal intended to] pick on one group [and] save money on the backs of welfare kids." He noted that the Joint Finance Committee had just approved a 30 percent increase in state payments to private attorneys under contract with the state's public defender office; if the state could help the lawyers representing the indigent, surely it could also help the indigent themselves. Republicans responded by pointing out that the state needed to pay the lawyers more or it would not be able to find anyone to serve as a public defender.

When the Joint Finance Committee voted on Republican efforts to reduce Governor Earl's welfare increases, it rejected them in virtually straight party-line votes (with only one Democratic dissent on the key vote and two on another). The action then shifted to the floor of the Assembly, where party lines were even tighter. The slight Democratic majority (52 percent) caucused on all budget matters, building a coalition (mainly by adding small pork barrel projects) that could defeat two Republican challenges in a straight party vote.[56]

This process was repeated the following week in the Senate, where the Democrats had a slightly larger (58 percent) majority over the Republicans. This time the bill with its welfare provisions passed by a 21–12 margin (three Republicans crossed over to support it, while one Democrat defected).[57] Informal discussions between the houses allowed them to reconcile differences and pass identical budgets by the last day of June.

The following year, the change in partisan balance produced a somewhat different outcome. After winning the governor's office in 1986, Thompson proposed cutting AFDC benefits and using the money for a job training program. Democratic control of the state legislature limited Thompson's success, however. The Joint Finance Committee went along with Thompson in eliminating a 1 percent

56. "Assembly Dems Stay Together on Budget," *Wisconsin State Journal,* June 16, 1985.
57. "At 4:30 a.m., Senate Approves State Budget," *Wisconsin State Journal,* June 24, 1985.

increase that was to take effect in April, but it refused to cut benefits by the additional 5 percent the governor wanted.

In the Senate, Democrats decided in a party caucus to establish their own $32.8 million welfare program, mainly for job training, education, and child care. Although $12.6 million of this amount was to come from the funds saved by eliminating the 1 percent benefit increase, the bulk was going to have to be raised from other state tax sources.[58] As usual, what was adopted in the majority caucus was left virtually untouched by the full Senate, as fifty-one out of fifty-two Republican floor amendments were rejected, including an attempt to cut AFDC benefits back by an additional 3 percent. The one amendment that was approved was to spend $75,000 on a ferry service in one Republican's district. The approval of this amendment was considered by some to be a blatant attempt to "buy" the Republican's vote on the overall budget, so the Democrats could label the budget "bipartisan." The attempt did not work; the Republican voted against the bill even after his amendment was adopted.[59]

The Politics of the Welfare Magnet

The Wisconsin case vividly illustrates several characteristics of state policymaking systems throughout the United States (see chapter 3 for further discussion). First, the welfare magnet debate in Wisconsin, as elsewhere, focused exclusively and misleadingly on the effect of welfare benefits on the in-migration of poor people. The effects on outward migration do not have the same political significance, and therefore both sides in the debate ignored one-half of the relevant information. Instead, those claiming the existence of a welfare magnet relied heavily on anecdotes about changes occurring in Wisconsin border towns, while those denying it relied on interview data about new welfare recipients' reasons for coming to Wisconsin.

58. David Stoeffler, "Welfare Reform Tied to Budget," *Wisconsin State Journal*, June 16, 1987.
59. David Stoeffler, "Senate Approves Budget," *Wisconsin State Journal*, June 19, 1987.

No matter how misleading the evidence relied upon in this debate, there was little doubt that the magnet issue affected the formulation of welfare policy. That Wisconsin's benefits were high was well known to both decisionmakers and the attentive public. The possible effect of high benefits on residential choice was debated, investigated, studied, and used as an issue in a gubernatorial campaign. Republicans regarded the issue as advantageous to them and consistently brought it to public view. Border-area Democrats defected to the Republican camp, and even Democratic Governor Earl conceded the plausibility of the Republican argument.

The case study also shows how the economy can have an important influence on welfare policy. As Wisconsin became more worried about its ability to compete effectively with other states for economic prosperity, it became more willing to cut welfare benefits, especially in favor of job training programs.

Not that cuts in welfare were easily carried out or especially large. Wisconsin's political culture had always emphasized using the public purse to help those whom economic progress had left behind. Even in a more fragile economic context, the instinct of the community to help its own did not fade away. Wisconsin's moralistic culture did have its boundaries, however. Like its mascot, the badger, Wisconsin tenaciously defended its own but was reluctant to succor those from outside the family.

Finally, welfare policy seems to have been shaped by political competition in the state. During the 1985–87 budget cycle, Governor Earl and his Democratic majority in the legislature were able to push through an increase in welfare benefits in spite of stiff opposition from the Republican majority (and the occasional Democratic defector). The Democratic legislature, probably sensing the political boundaries for raising benefits, did reduce Governor Earl's initial recommendations but approved an increase nonetheless. The following year's gubernatorial campaign changed the balance. Republican Tommy Thompson attacked Earl's welfare policies and apparently convinced the voters that the Democratic incumbent's policies were adversely affecting the state's business climate. But Governor Thompson's success with the voters did not immediately reverse state welfare policy. Since Thompson's proposed benefit cuts went against the wishes of the Democratic majority in the legislature, benefits were never cut. However, because they were not increased enough to keep pace with the cost of living, in real terms Wisconsin's monthly welfare benefits (AFDC plus food stamps) for a family of four declined from about $760 to $720 between 1980 and 1985.

Wisconsin is an unusually generous state. Neither its welfare system nor its politics are typical of other states', and many in Wisconsin are proud of its Progressive heritage. But if Wisconsin is so independent-minded, it is all the more significant that it became the site of a major debate over the effect of welfare benefits on the residential choices of the poor. If even a moderately prosperous state with political institutions and cultural traditions that support welfare ends up reducing benefits to preserve its business climate, to what extent are other states also tempted to cut welfare benefits in order to avoid becoming welfare magnets? An answer to this question requires the more quantitative analysis to which we now turn.

Chapter 3

State Welfare Policies and Residential Choices

THE WISCONSIN experience may have been singular. It is an unusually progressive state with a propensity for policy innovation. It is distinctive in that few states are smaller, high-benefit states located next to a larger low-benefit state with a large welfare-dependent population. It is unique in having a commission investigate the reasons welfare recipients gave for moving to the state.

Yet the distinctive elements in the Wisconsin case may be less significant than those it shares with other state policymaking systems. For example, it was not the only state in which welfare-induced migration was recognized as an issue. The same topic arose at about the same time in Texas, a low-benefit southern state with a more traditional political culture. In the words of the *Houston Post*:

> Lean pickings in Texas prompt many people on public assistance to move to other states where the welfare payments are higher. . . . [King Cox, regional director for public assistance with the Texas Department of Human Services,] said that's his perception. . . . People from other states often call and ask the level of welfare payments, then say there is no way they would move to Texas.[1]

The article invited public comment. In one reader's view, the paper

1. Brenda Sapino, "Official Says Welfare Benefits Discourage Relocating to Texas," *Houston Post,* February 22, 1987, p. 4D.

had for once printed "a pleasant and encouraging news item." Another reader invited "Texas Democrats" to move to "New York," which "ranks first in welfare payments." To which the editor replied: "You may jest but some recipients in low-welfare states do migrate to states which make higher payments."[2]

If Texans thought welfare recipients might choose to live in New York, the same thought occurred to New York politicians. In the midst of a 1981 debate over benefit increases, Republican State Comptroller and gubernatorial aspirant Edward V. Regan issued a report purporting to show that New York's high public assistance benefits discouraged recipients from seeking work elsewhere and hampered the state in its competition for business with other parts of the country. Although the comptroller said that his report "should not be viewed as a recommendation for or against a benefit increase," Lieutenant Governor Mario Cuomo, also contemplating higher office, denounced the report for relying on the "nonempirical assumption that poor people migrate to New York because of its benefit levels."[3] This issue also surfaced in Massachusetts politics in 1990. A conservative Democratic candidate for governor, John Silber, suggested that the number of Cambodians in Lowell seemed to be affected by state welfare policy. Liberal politicians and state welfare officials accused Silber of racist language and denied that welfare policy affected residential choices.

If welfare-induced migration has been an issue in states as diverse as Texas, New York, and Massachusetts, then the factors affecting welfare policy in Wisconsin may also account for state welfare policies more generally. In Wisconsin, for example, the pressure for reducing welfare benefits became more intense as the number of poor people increased. Do changes in the percentages of poor people affect welfare policy in most states? Also, the pressures on the Wisconsin economy seemed to be influencing the welfare debate. Do welfare benefits in most states depend on the state's economic

2. *Houston Post,* March 4, 1987, p. 1B.

3. Richard J. Meislin, "Comptroller Steps Up His Attack on Increasing State Welfare Aid," *New York Times,* February 3, 1981, p. B6; and Lena Williams, "Cuomo Counters Attack by Regan on Welfare Rise," *New York Times,* February 4, 1981, p. B3.

well-being? The issue in Wisconsin was highly partisan and shaped by electoral strategies. Does the nature of political competition make a difference in most states? Wisconsin's progressive political culture helped to sustain a high benefit level; does this factor influence policies elsewhere as well?

Theories of State Policymaking

The influences that affect state policymaking have been debated at some length. There are two main schools of thought. The dominant approach has been based on the assumption that politicians are responding to political forces within the state. This approach can be formalized by constructing a model that assumes that state officials are designing policies in order to attract the support of the median voter. Within this framework, policy outcomes can be shaped by political factors such as political culture, party competition, and degree of electoral mobilization because these factors help determine which groups are best able to mobilize voter support for their position. By altering the composition of the voting public, these factors directly influence the policy choices of political leaders. In Wisconsin, for example, the moralistic political culture and intense party competition helped mobilize liberal support for higher welfare benefits.

Policies can also be shaped by such social and economic variables as per capita income, degree of urbanization, and population density. In early research on state policy these variables were misconceived as purely economic factors that determined public policy independently of a state's political system, and a good deal of debate was devoted to the relative importance of economic *versus* political determinants of public policy. But, as Plotnick and Winters have made clear, "The conflict between economic and political explanations of redistribution is an artificial one."[4] Within the framework of the median-voter model, economic variables can best be under-

---

4. Robert D. Plotnick and Richard F. Winters, "A Politico-Economic Theory of Income Redistribution," *American Political Science Review*, vol. 79 (June 1985), pp. 458–73, quote on p. 471.

stood as indicators of voter preferences within a state.[5] For example, rural voters are expected to demand more roads per capita, increased population density is said to result in demands for more police and fire protection, and higher per capita income is thought to generate demand for higher-quality public services (to keep pace with greater consumption in the private sector). As long as one realizes that economic variables help identify political predispositions, it is not difficult to incorporate them within a median-voter model of policy formation.

Much of the popularity of this model is due to its flexibility. Virtually any relationship between a social or economic variable and a policy outcome can be included in the model simply by making a series of plausible but unverified inferences about the way a particular economic or social condition affects voter preferences. Indeed, different studies using the median-voter model have made exactly opposite inferences about these effects in order to account for disparate findings.

The instance most relevant here is the relationship between state poverty rates and welfare benefits. In some uses of the median-voter model it is assumed that the higher the proportion of poor people in a state, the greater the demand for welfare services and thus the higher the level of welfare benefits.[6] But other assumptions about the relationship between these two variables are just as readily incorporated within the median-voter model. It may be assumed that as poverty in a state increases, so does the tax burden on the nonpoor, whose opposition to high levels of welfare provision will accordingly become more intense.[7] If these inferences are correct, then increases in poverty rates will lower benefit levels, not increase them.

The virtue of the median-voter model is that it can account for

5. As Plotnick and Winters point out, these economic factors can also indirectly influence policy by affecting the values of such political variables as party competition or a state's political culture. "A Politico-Economic Theory."

6. Sam Peltzman, "The Growth of Government," *Journal of Law and Economics,* vol. 23 (October 1980), pp. 209–87.

7. Edward M. Gramlich and Deborah S. Laren, "Migration and Income Redistribution Responsibilities," *Journal of Human Resources,* vol. 19 (Fall 1984), pp. 489–511; and Plotnick and Winters, "A Politico-Economic Theory."

either set of empirical findings. But this very flexibility also limits its utility for empirical research. Precisely because it is so accommodating, it comes very close to being nothing more than a set of tautological statements. If rising poverty rates can be said, other things being equal, to cause vote-conscious politicians *either* to raise *or* to lower benefit levels, then the model has no predictive capacity at all. It simply incorporates whatever empirical relationship happens to be observed.[8]

A second approach emphasizes that states are engaged in economic competition and assumes that state policymakers attempt to enhance the economic performance of their state.[9] This view gives more precise predictions about welfare policy choice. In pursuit of high economic performance, policymakers design public policies to appeal to firms, productive workers, and investors. This approach can be formalized by constructing a model that assumes that state policymakers seek to maximize state property values (in much the same way that executives of a firm are assumed to be interested in maximizing profits). Unless policymakers hold to this objective, their states risk economic decline, the loss of tax revenues, and, in the extreme case, the inability to raise capital funds in the bond market (just as a firm that does not maximize profit risks devaluation of its stock, takeover attempts, and bankruptcy).

These value-maximizing policymakers can be expected to restrict welfare benefits because a benefit level that is too high will increase the size of the state's poor population. This does not necessarily mean that value-maximizing politicians will eliminate welfare provision altogether, however; even in eighteenth century England local counties provided some assistance to their own poor, though they made strenuous efforts to make sure outsiders did not poach on their provision.[10] In a much wealthier and more liberal modern

8. Presumably one might try to determine which inference is correct by ascertaining the direction and the intensity of the preferences of both the poor and the nonpoor. But this has never been done, could be done only at great cost, and, even if it were done, would not resolve the matter because citizens' true preferences, as revealed by their behavior, might be different from the preferences stated in an anonymous interview.

9. Paul E. Peterson, *City Limits* (University of Chicago Press, 1981), pp. 17–38.

10. Residency requirements have an ancient if not altogether honorable origin

society, one expects that all states will provide some welfare services simply because most citizens would not want to live and work in a state that totally ignored its poor.[11] Nonetheless, the desire of any one state to avoid excess responsibility for the nation's poor is likely to lead to a lower level of welfare provision than would occur if policy were determined nationally.

The level of welfare benefits is not likely to be uniform across states. Policymakers are more likely to assist the poor if their state's taxable wealth is already high relative to that in other states, because a higher level of welfare provision can be offered at tax rates at or below the level pertaining in other jurisdictions. The needy can be more easily accommodated without giving productive firms and citizens incentives to move elsewhere. But if benefits become too much higher than those in other states, policymakers will act to reduce them in order not to attract excessive numbers of poor people from other states. And if poverty rates in a state are high and increasing, value-maximizing policymakers will be even more inclined to reduce benefit levels.

The value-maximizing model has been criticized for placing too

---

in the English Poor Law. In the seventeenth and eighteenth centuries, English parishes were able to provide widely varying levels of relief by ensuring that each parish provided only for its own poor. Migration was prohibited, and "constables on the main roads sometimes spent the whole of their time transporting paupers. . . . In fact, the history of the Poor Laws is largely an account of efforts to deny support to, and to deport, the itinerant poor. Cruel instances abound of whippings, the splitting of families, and the expulsion of widows and unwed mothers." Charles C. Brown and Wallace E. Oates, "Assistance to the Poor in a Federal System," University of Maryland, Department of Economics, 1986, p. 27.

11. The difference between states and local governments that are within metropolitan governments might clarify this point. At the local level it is feasible to exclude low-income people from a suburb, school district, or other small political entity even though they provide unskilled labor used by the overall economy of the metropolitan area upon whose prosperity the small, exclusive political entity depends. Under these circumstances local governments can be expected to provide virtually no welfare assistance and use even more direct exclusionary tactics in order to maintain property values. At the state level, such extremes are less likely because states typically include one or more fairly complete metropolitan economies. Because this necessarily entails the presence of some low-income residents, state policies cannot be designed to bar poor people from all services. Quite apart from political considerations, such a policy in an industrial society is probably not feasible, socially or economically.

little weight on the role of group and electoral influences on state policymaking, for exaggerating the effect that state policies have on the location decisions of both firms and families, and for overestimating the sensitivity of policymakers to economic constraints. If the model has the virtue of generating quite specific hypotheses, its weakness is that it ignores variables that presumably have significant policy effects.

One way of reconciling the value-maximizing and median-voter models is to assume that economic conditions in a state have significant political consequences.[12] If voters judge political incumbents according to how well the state economy is performing, then one way political leaders can gain votes is by promoting economic growth or, more generally, by maximizing property values. Economic prosperity need not be the only factor that politicians take into account when formulating politically popular welfare policies. Their calculations may also be affected by the degree of party competition in the state, the extent to which low-income citizens are politically mobilized, or the liberality of the state's political culture. When formulated in these terms, the question is no longer a matter of which model is correct. Instead, the two models are combined in order to generate more specific hypotheses than those ordinarily generated by the median-voter model. In particular, the property-maximizing model is used to specify the vote-maximizing model by identifying a set of economic factors that have significant political consequences. Instead of treating voters as simply liberal or conservative, rich or poor, or altruistic or self-interested, as do many applications of the median-voter model, this conceptualization regards the median voter as economically sensitive in just the way most studies have shown voters to be. If a state is doing well

12. Morris P. Fiorina, *Retrospective Voting in American National Elections* (Yale University Press, 1981); Douglas A. Hibbs, Jr., *The American Political Economy: Macroeconomics and Electoral Politics* (Harvard University Press, 1987); D. Roderick Kiewiet, *Macroeconomics and Micropolitics: The Electoral Effects of Economic Issues* (University of Chicago Press, 1983); and Samuel Kernell, *Going Public: New Strategies of Presidential Leadership* (Washington: Congressional Quarterly, 1986).

economically, incumbents tend to be rewarded. If a state is suffering economic decline, voters are more likely to call for a change.[13]

When the median-voter model is specified in this way, welfare benefits are no longer expected to rise with increases in the size of the low-income population. Instead, it is expected that as the poor population in the state increases (relative to its size elsewhere), the more prosperous, taxpaying citizens become more concerned about both the rising cost of welfare and the adverse neighborhood effects. In Kenosha, Wisconsin, for example, the issue was not just increases in state welfare expenditures but the effects of increased poverty on local services and neighborhood property values.

Most studies of the effects of welfare benefits on interstate migration have ignored these political issues. Instead, they have typically taken welfare benefits as a given and then examined their effects on residential choices. Their findings have depended mainly on the period during which the data they analyzed was collected. The first and largest wave of studies was undertaken in the late 1960s and early 1970s in the context of the debate over the family assistance plan proposed by President Richard Nixon. The administration justified its proposal to standardize benefits partly on the grounds that large differences in welfare benefits were encouraging the movement of potential recipients from low-benefit to high-benefit states. Critics responded by pointing to studies showing that the amount of interstate migration that could be attributed to differential welfare benefits was either statistically or substantively insignificant (see appendix A). The data for these studies were collected in the 1950s and 1960s, when many states did not provide welfare benefits until newcomers had met a twelve-month residency requirement.[14] But in 1969 the Supreme Court (in *Shapiro* v. *Thompson*) ruled that states could no longer constitutionally deny benefits to new residents.[15] Eligible recipients could now receive benefits as soon as they moved into the state and as quickly as

13. John E. Chubb, "Institutions, the Economy, and the Dynamics of State Elections," *American Political Science Review*, vol. 82 (March 1988) pp. 133–54.
14. Brown and Oates, "Assistance to the Poor in a Federal System."
15. 394 U.S. 618 (1969).

applications could be processed. Consequently, differences in state welfare benefits may have had a more substantial effect on residential choice after 1970 than before.

Two important studies using data collected since 1970 both reach conclusions at odds with the bulk of the earlier research.[16] Although their findings suggest that the conclusions reached at the time of the debate over the family assistance plan may no longer apply, each study has limitations that leaves the issue unresolved. Blank's study shows that the combined effect of differential wages and welfare benefits is to induce migration from one region to another. However, her study does not disentangle the independent effects of wages and benefits, combines the fifty states into ten regions (thereby reducing the precision with which the welfare benefit variable is measured), and does not take into account the possibility of simultaneous effects of benefits and migration on each other.

Gramlich and Laren, in addition to supporting Blank's individual-level findings, develop a model using aggregate data to estimate the simultaneous relationship between welfare benefits and the recipient population. They find that the effect of welfare benefits on migration is strong and significant. Their presentation of the determinants of benefit levels, however, includes only two economic factors: the price of AFDC benefits and per capita income. Differences in "tastes, institutions, and other factors" among the states are simply incorporated into the intercept term.[17] By attributing the whole weight of their theoretical model to economic variables, they do not build on the findings of the more subtle analyses of welfare policymaking described above.

Research Design

Earlier evidence that welfare did not influence interstate migration is being reexamined and revised in the light of newer data and better techniques. However, the new literature on interstate mi-

---

16. Rebecca M. Blank, "The Impact of State Economic Differentials on Household Welfare and Labor Force Behavior," *Journal of Public Economics,* vol. 28 (October 1985), pp. 25–58; and Gramlich and Laren, "Migration and Income Redistribution."

17. Gramlich and Laren, "Migration and Income Redistribution," p. 494.

gration has yet to be integrated into a more comprehensive model linking migration and state policymaking. We turn now to this task. We present a model that estimates differences in welfare benefits derived from the vote- and value-maximizing theories previously outlined; a model of economic and policy factors affecting interstate migration of the poor; and an approach that links the policymaking and migration models. The empirical indicators and sources for the data used in the analysis are given in appendix B.

Benefit Levels

Studies have measured the policy differences among the states by using such indicators as the average payments per recipient, maximum AFDC benefits for a family of three, and combined AFDC cash and food stamp benefits for a family of four. Statistically, it makes very little difference which is chosen. All these measures of welfare benefits are highly correlated, and they yield similar results in regression estimations.[18] However, as a theoretical matter, the combination of AFDC cash and food stamp payments is the best choice. Combined cash and food stamp guarantees are the broadest available measure of welfare policy and thus the one likely to be most salient to potential recipients.[19] Also, unlike actual benefits, maximum welfare guarantees are directly controlled by policymakers.[20]

18. Controlling for the time period, the partial correlations between three- and four-person maximum AFDC payments, three- and four-person combined AFDC cash and food stamp benefits, and average cash payments per family were at least 0.87. All but the average cash payments per family approached 1.0.

19. In 1983, 83 percent of families receiving AFDC participated in a "food stamp or donated food program." *Background Material and Data on Programs within the Jurisdiction of the Committee on Ways and Means,* Committee Print, House Committee on Ways and Means, 99 Cong. 2 sess. (Government Printing Office, 1986) p. 393.

20. The variable that is most directly controlled by state policymakers is the maximum level of cash benefits. The simultaneous effects of this variable are interpreted in appendix C. But since the maximum combined cash and food stamp benefit is also indirectly set at the state level and is of greatest interest to recipients, we have selected it as the best measure of the simultaneous effect of poverty rates and benefit levels on each other. Both indicators are preferred over average family payments, which are not solely determined by policymakers since they depend in part on the conditions of recipients. See Plotnick and Winters, "A Politico-Economic

Potential Welfare Recipients

One of the most difficult problems to solve in studies of the relationships between welfare policy and residential choice is how to measure the migration-caused net change in the size of the population most likely to be affected by welfare policy. In order to determine the effects of policy on residential choice, one needs to measure changes in a group's size that are simply due to interstate migration, as distinct from changes in the characteristics of individuals living within a state. Most of the studies using pre-1970 data used the percentage of blacks as an indicator of the group at risk of becoming welfare dependent.[21] The advantage of this measure is that racial designations seldom change. Any change in racial composition that cannot be attributed to differential birth or mortality rates must therefore be due to migration. But the percentage of blacks residing in a state is still an inadequate measure of a welfare-sensitive population. Eighty-five percent of the black population did not receive AFDC payments in 1985, and more than one-half of AFDC recipients were not black.[22] Because of these limitations we shall not place primary reliance on findings using this variable. Nonetheless, we shall report results using this indicator as a check on the reliability of our findings using poverty-rate data.

Another widely used measure that has quite the opposite virtues and limitations is the percentage of the population receiving welfare

---

Theory." Southwick agrees: "Because the effect of work (earnings) is included in the average payment, potential benefits are a better measure of that incentive to migrate which is due to the welfare programs. It represents a cushion or minimum level of subsistence available to the unemployed migrant." Lawrence Southwick, Jr., "Public Welfare Programs and Recipient Migration," *Growth and Change*, vol. 12 (October 1981), p. 22.

21. See appendix A: Dejong and Donnelly, "Public Welfare and Migration"; Kain and Schafer, "Income Maintenance, Migration and Regional Growth"; Cebula, Kohn, and Vedder, "Some Determinants of Interstate Migration"; Lansing and Mueller, *Geographic Mobility of Labor*; Long, "Poverty Status and Receipt of Welfare"; Reischauer, "Impact of the Welfare System"; Sommers and Suits, "Analysis of Net Migration"; and Southwick, "Public Welfare Programs."

22. Authors' calculations from *Background Material*, Committee Print, p. 392.

° blacks, it is a direct measure
___me maintenance policies.
_e of the measure is that it is so sensitive to welfare
the size of the within-state recipient population may
as a result of policy change. As benefits increase, more
_uals become eligible for assistance and more may find it
_h their while to incur the information costs, bureaucratic
_sles, and public stigmas that accompany an application for
_enefits.[24] As benefits decrease, eligibility becomes more restricted
and the incentive for applying declines. Because welfare policy
changes can affect the size of the resident welfare population in
these ways, it is difficult to distinguish with aggregate data any of
these within-state effects from changes in interstate migration
patterns the policy may have caused.[25]

The measure that we have selected—changes in the poverty rate
within a state—has its own deficiencies, but these are outweighed
by its advantages.[26] First, it is a much better proxy for the welfare-
sensitive population than is the percentage of blacks. About 40
percent of the population officially described as living in poverty
receives AFDC payments at any given time. Many poor people, not

23. Gramlich and Laren, "Migration and Income Redistribution"; and Southwick,
"Public Welfare Programs," use several different indicators, including this one.

24. N. A. Barr and R. E. Hall, "The Probability of Dependence on Public
Assistance," Economica, vol. 48 (May 1981), pp. 109–23; Robert Moffitt, "An Economic
Model of Welfare Stigma," American Economic Review, vol. 73 (December 1983), pp.
1023–35; Moffitt, "Historical Growth in Participation in Aid to Families with
Dependent Children: Was There a Structural Shift?" Journal of Post Keynesian
Economics, vol. 9 (Spring 1987), pp. 347–63; and C. T. Brehm and T. R. Saving, "The
Demand for General Assistance Payments," American Economic Review, vol. 54
(December 1964), pp. 1002–18.

25. Gramlich and Laren, "Migration and Income Redistribution," attempt to
distinguish within-state from between-state effects statistically, but the effort
requires heroic assumptions and the results are counterintuitive (between-state
effects exceed within-state effects). We report the results of our effort to predict
changes in the percentage of welfare recipients in appendix C. In our view, no firm
conclusions can be drawn from these data.

26. We are aware of only one, now quite outdated, study that has examined the
effects of welfare policy on migration of the poor: F. B. Glantz, "The Determinants
of Intermetropolitan Migration of the Economically Disadvantaged," Federal Reserve
Bank of Boston Research Report no. 52, January 1973. He found that differences in
benefit levels affected migration rates in the 1950s but not in the 1960s.

just welfare recipients, are likely to be sensitive to changes in welfare policies. Contrary to the myth that the welfare system affects only a well-defined "underclass" consisting of welfare recipients dependent on income maintenance programs for long periods, most of those who receive welfare in any given year leave the rolls within a year.[27] In other words, the rolls are continuously churning, thereby involving a much larger percentage of the low-income population than is usually realized.

Although the poverty rate is a good indicator of the population most susceptible to changes in welfare policy, its weakness is that changes in this variable can occur for reasons other than interstate migration, our central theoretical concern. For one thing, if employment opportunities and earnings levels change within a state, within-state poverty may change without any migration occurring. We have addressed this problem by including appropriate controls for changes in state economic conditions.

The second problem is less easily addressed. It may be that changes in welfare policies themselves affect the size of the resident poor population. Two possible effects may occur. First, in several states, welfare benefits combined with earned income could lift a family above the poverty line. For example, in California, the most generous state, a family of four in 1985 could have earned $6,666, provided that child care and work-related expenses equaled that amount, and still receive the maximum of $8,376 per year. The combination of benefits and earned income could technically lift the family above the poverty line (which was $10,614).[28] This rarely happens, however; 80 percent of families receiving AFDC benefits in 1988 did not report any other source of income. Only 2.1 percent

27. Mary Jo Bane and David T. Ellwood, "The Dynamics of Dependence: The Routes to Self-Sufficiency," Department of Health and Human Services, Contract no. HHS-100-82-0038 (Cambridge, Mass.: Urban Systems Research and Engineering, June 1983).

28. Authors' calculations based on data from Christine Ross and Sheldon Danziger, "Poverty Rates by States, 1978–83: Estimates from the Annual Current Population Surveys," University of Wisconsin, Institute for Research on Poverty, March 1986.

of women enrolled in the program had full-time jobs, with another 4.2 percent working part time.[29]

The second possibility is that increases in benefit levels may actually increase the size of the poor population. Although studies differ, there is some evidence that income maintenance policies encourage the formation of female-headed households, the demographic group at greatest risk of being poor.[30] Studies also differ as to the extent that higher benefits reduce incentives to work and, as a result, discourage recipients from obtaining entry-level jobs in which they can acquire work skills that lead to higher earning potential and escape from poverty conditions.[31] To the extent that these relationships obtain, it is conceivable that poverty rates could change within a state as a function of changes in welfare policy. But the evidence on these effects is so mixed and uncertain that it is unlikely that either factor significantly biases the results reported below. (See discussion on pages 79–80.)

The Time Period

Neither the effect of benefits on migration nor the effect of migration on benefit levels is likely to occur instantaneously. Poor people will only gradually hear about changes in benefit levels in other states, and their life circumstances may not allow them to move immediately. Similarly, policymakers will only gradually acquire information about changes in the size of the low-income population, and efforts to adjust policy accordingly will work their way slowly through political channels.

29. *Overview of Entitlement Programs,* Committee Print, House Committee on Ways and Means, 101 Cong. 2 sess. (GPO, 1990), p. 580.

30. Robert D. Plotnick, "Welfare and Other Determinants of Teenage Out-of-Wedlock Childbearing," University of Washington, School of Public Affairs, 1987; for a contrary finding, see David T. Ellwood and Mary Jo Bane, "The Impact of AFDC on Family Structure and Living Arrangements," *Research in Labor Economics,* vol. 7 (1985), pp. 137–207.

31. Sheldon Danziger, Robert Haveman, and Robert Plotnick, "How Income Transfer Programs Affect Work, Savings, and the Income Distribution: A Critical Review," *Journal of Economic Literature,* vol. 19 (September 1981), pp. 975–1028.

In constructing a data set that took into account the sluggishness with which both human migration and political decisions respond to environmental change, we organized our data into three time periods consisting of five years each: 1970–75, 1975–80, and 1980–85.[32] Although the selection of time periods was determined in good part by the availability of data about poverty levels and other demographic conditions, these data constraints did not force us to make particularly restrictive assumptions. Changes in the distribution of poverty occur slowly, and states only occasionally adjust benefit levels. Five-year periods may not perfectly capture the lags between changes in welfare and poverty, but they should be long enough to observe any connection that does exist.[33] We use data beginning in 1970 because only after the 1969 Supreme Court ruling (*Shapiro* v. *Thompson*) could poor people move freely and still remain immediately eligible for welfare benefits.

In the selection of predictor variables, we usually had the choice of using level variables measured at the beginning of the five-year period or variables that measured changes over the same five-year period as the changes in poverty rates and benefit levels occurred. The choice depended on whether theoretical considerations led us to believe that effects would take place immediately or over a longer term. Level variables are preferable if effects are likely to be delayed; change variables are preferred if their effect is expected almost immediately. As we discuss each predictor variable, we will explain why we chose one that measured a level, a change in level, or the interaction between a level and a change in levels.

The Unit of Analysis

Our units of analysis consist of the forty-eight contiguous states plus the District of Columbia for each of the three time periods

32. We were unable to obtain all of our data for exactly the same year. When this was not possible we used data from the closest available time, which was within one year in all except two variables. See appendix B for details.

33. An alternative analytical approach is to use annual data that lag predictor variables for varying time periods, thus permitting an empirical assessment of the time it takes for a response to the lagged effect to occur. Since poverty data were available only at five-year intervals, we could not pursue this analytic strategy.

specified above, a total of 147 potential cases.[34] The state is obviously the best unit of analysis for estimating the effects of poverty rates on state welfare policies, but it has certain disadvantages for estimating the effects of welfare benefits on interstate migration. Survey data on the migration of individuals can directly ascertain whether welfare recipients have migrated across state boundaries and need not infer (as we must) that changes in poverty rates associated with changes in benefit levels are a function of residential choice (rather than a function of changes in family composition or willingness to work). We chose not to use individual-level data because the state-by-state samples within existing data sets are small and unrepresentative of the states' populations.[35]

A Simultaneous Model of Change

In order to see whether the factors that influenced welfare policy in Wisconsin were important in other states, we constructed a model

34. Incomplete data reduced the actual observations by a few cases. Exact numbers are given in the tables. This is the first study of welfare and migration based on pooled data from three time periods. By pooling the data, we increase our sample size and obtain more reliable estimates. This analytic technique is acceptable provided that the relationships among the variables do not change significantly over time, a requirement that this analysis meets; that is, the intercept differs across periods but the coefficients for the explanatory variables do not. To allow the intercept to vary, dummy variables for the periods were entered. All proved to have highly significant coefficients and are presented in our results. To test the hypothesis that the coefficients are stable over time, all explanatory variables were multiplied by the period dummy variables and the equations were reestimated. The t-statistics computed for the new variables indicated that each coefficient was consistent from period to period (at the 0.05 percent level of probability); an F-statistic indicated that the entire set of coefficients was also consistent over time. See Eric A. Hanushek and John E. Jackson, *Statistical Methods for Social Scientists* (Academic Press, 1977), p. 128.

35. The two recent studies using individual–level data cannot be accepted as definitive. Gramlich and Laren ("Migration and Income Redistribution") do not control for the effects of wages, employment opportunities, or other relevant variables, and Blank ("Impact of State Economic Differentials") does not distinguish between welfare and wage effects but combines them together into a single variable conceptualized as potential income effects. In addition, both studies depend upon small samples and cannot estimate the simultaneous effects of benefits on policy and vice versa. Both nonetheless conclude that the effects of welfare policy on migration since 1970 have been both substantively and statistically significant, results consistent with our findings.

that estimated both the determinants of changes in poverty rates among the states and the determinants of changes in welfare benefits. We shall first discuss the part of the model used to estimate the changes in benefit levels and then discuss the part used to estimate changes in poverty rates.

Changing Welfare Benefits

Consistent with our policymaking model, our hypothesis is that welfare policies are influenced not only by a state's economic resources and its need to compete with other states for productive capital and labor but also by cultural norms that make welfare-related political demands more legitimate in some states than others and by political institutions that give pro- or antiwelfare groups more influence in some states than in others.

The equation we used to estimate changes in benefit levels is:

$$(1) \quad \Delta B_{it} = a_0 + a_1 (P_{ij}\Delta P_{it}) + a_2 B_{ij} + a_3 PI_{ij} + a_4 T_{ij} + a_5 C_{ij} + a_6 P_{2it} + a_7 P_{3it} + e_{it},$$

where

ΔB = change in welfare benefits;

P = poverty as a percentage of the population;

ΔP = change in poverty levels;

B = welfare benefit levels;

PI = levels of political competition and participation;

T = levels of tax effort;

C = levels of tax capacity;

P_2 = period two (1975–1980), dummy variable;

P_3 = period three (1980–1985), dummy variable;

$a_0 \ldots_7$ = coefficients;

e = residual;

i = lower 48 states and the District of Columbia;

j = year, where j = 1, 2, or 3, and 1 = 1970, 2 = 1975, and 3 = 1980;

t = time period, where t = 1, 2, or 3, and 1 = 1970–75; 2 = 1975–80; and 3 = 1980–85.

Poverty. If the Wisconsin experience can be generalized, it can be hypothesized that high poverty levels would gradually induce policymakers to reduce lower benefit levels over time. Policymakers can be expected to calculate that having a large number of low-income people would strain state-provided social services, hurt property values, and force politically unpopular tax increases. As a result, the presence of a sizable poor population can be expected to generate pressure to cut benefits. We also hypothesized that policymakers might be sensitive to changes in poverty levels. If poverty levels were rising, pressure to cut benefits would immediately increase. To test these hypotheses, we specified our model in two different ways. In one equation, initial poverty levels and changes in poverty rates were both entered; in the second, poverty levels at the end of the period were used as indicators of policymakers' expectations of what poverty levels would be. (This expectations term is equivalent to poverty levels at the beginning of the period times the rate of change in poverty during the period, both of which policymakers could estimate with a fair degree of accuracy.) Preliminary analysis suggested that neither hypothesis could be rejected. Because multicollinearity among the variables precluded testing both hypotheses within one model, we chose the expectations model because it was theoretically more satisfying and produced a better fit. (The results from the equation in which initial poverty terms and the change in poverty levels were entered separately can be found in appendix C.)

Economic conditions. Both the Wisconsin case and other studies suggest that a complete model of welfare policymaking also needs to take into account additional factors affecting the economic well-being of the state.[36] We hypothesized that the more prosperous the state, the less constrained policymakers were when it came to financing social welfare programs. The same tax rate will generate more revenue per capita, making it easier to finance redistributive programs without providing disincentives to firms and taxpaying households. We used indicators of the level of economic prosperity in the state at the beginning of the period instead of changes in the

---

36. Thomas R. Dye, *Politics, Economics, and the Public: Policy Outcomes in the American States* (Rand McNally, 1966); Peterson, *City Limits*; and Plotnick and Winters, "A Politico-Economic Theory."

state economy during the period. The level variables were preferred because we assumed that policymakers react slowly to environmental change and that economic factors will influence policy only gradually over a five-year period. We originally included unemployment rates, employment levels, per capita income, and tax capacity in our analysis; in the final equation we retained only the one whose coefficients remained stable and significant: tax capacity, a summary indicator of the overall taxable wealth of a state.[37]

Political institutions. The Wisconsin case indicated that institutions structuring the state's electoral politics can influence state welfare policy. Other studies have reached similar conclusions. Drawing on the work of V. O. Key, Jennings has observed that "close interparty competition provides strong incentives for both parties to formulate policies for the benefit of the 'have-nots' "; if politicians love the poor, it is because there are so many of them who potentially can vote.[38] Without two-party competition, electoral politics in the United States revolves around personal factions lacking durable policy commitments. Those with money and status gain influence at the expense of those whose main political resource is the vote. But party competition alone cannot explain variations in state welfare policies: it needs to be found in combination with other factors if it is to have policy consequences. As Jennings concludes, "the generosity of a state's social welfare policies depends upon the organization and mobilization of the lower classes in the electoral process," which requires more than just party competitiveness.[39] Because these institutional conditions influencing wel-

---

37. It might be thought that omission of a level measure of per capita income enhanced the predictive value of our indicator of poverty. Appendix C demonstrates that results do not change significantly when the variable is included, although the sign of the income variable has a direction that is inconsistent with other research (Gramlich and Laren, "Migration and Income Redistribution"). Because this could be due to multicollinearity with both the tax capacity and the poverty variables (0.67 and −0.64, respectively), we did not include the income variable in the final equation. Other variables not included in the analysis are discussed in appendix D.

38. Edward T. Jennings, Jr., "Competition, Constituencies, and Welfare Policies in American States," *American Political Science Review*, vol. 73 (June 1979), p. 415. The reference is to V. O. Key, Jr., *Southern Politics in State and Nation* (Alfred A. Knopf, 1949).

39. "Competition, Constituencies, and Welfare Policies," p. 416. Jennings reviews

fare policy appear to be interrelated, we constructed an index that combined measures of party competition and class mobilization. The partisan balance between the Democratic and Republican parties in the state legislature was chosen as the best indicator of the degree of institutionalized party competition.[40] Measuring class mobilization was more difficult, since good data on the effects of socioeconomic background on voter turnout and partisan choice are lacking at the state level. As a substitute, we used voter turnout in gubernatorial elections.[41] Its selection is based on the assumption that in states characterized by factional, personal politics, voter turnout will generally be low even when "competition" between "parties" is high. Conversely, states with high voter turnouts typically have higher class mobilization and are more likely to have at least one party in favor of broadening the welfare state.[42]

---

the literature developing the competitive-parties hypothesis. In his study of eight states, he found that states with clear class divisions between parties generally had higher benefits and that when the party representing the lower class dominated (or at least achieved a split in) the legislature and the governor's office, it provided welfare more generously.

40. As a summary of many individual races at frequent intervals, it is a better measure of general party competition than gubernatorial elections, which are less frequent and more idiosyncratic. Because it involves state offices, it is more representative of party competition regarding state issues than congressional elections would be. We are grateful to John E. Chubb for providing quantitative data on state political institutions used in this chapter.

41. Available data on turnout rates for state legislative races are very incomplete; data on gubernatorial elections seemed the best substitute. Many states did not have gubernatorial elections during the first year of our periods, so we used data from the election closest to that year.

42. Initially we entered variables representing party competition and voter mobilization separately. Neither significantly influenced changes in welfare benefit levels, although all coefficients had the expected sign. The joint effect of party competition and class mobilization, measured by multiplying the two terms together, proved to be a more stable and significant predictor (a result anticipated by Jennings's work). This variable reaches its maximum value when there is a 100 percent voter turnout in gubernatorial elections and the state legislature is almost exactly split between the Republican and Democratic parties. We also included a third variable measuring control over state government by the party representing low-income groups. We combined data on control of the governor's office with data on which party had a majority in the state legislature; in each case we assumed that the Democratic party would be more sympathetic to demands for higher welfare benefits. (If the state Senate and House were split, legislative control was defined as a simple majority of all legislators.) However, this measure did not add to the explanatory

Political culture. The state's political culture is a third factor expected to influence welfare policy. Both the Wisconsin case and a number of earlier studies suggest that states exemplifying moralistic political cultures will be more willing to tax themselves to pay for social welfare programs simply because they believe it is the right thing to do.[43] The best available measure of this aspect of a state's political culture is how much a state, given its economic resources, is willing to tax itself. We hypothesized that the higher a state's tax effort, the less we would expect it to cut welfare benefits even when controlling for other political and economic changes. Because culture is expected to shape policy only gradually, we used a level variable, rather than a change variable, to estimate its effect.

State "exposure" to potential migration. The debate over the Wisconsin welfare magnet suggested another hypothesis: namely, that the welfare benefit level in each state at the beginning of each period would affect the extent to which benefits changed during the period. If states are engaged in economic competition, we would be surprised if any state allowed its benefits to "get out of line." Just as states can be expected to cut benefits if they see that in-migration is occurring, we anticipate that they will reduce benefits if they are high enough that policymakers fear in-migration might take place. Conversely, below-average states may cut their benefits less or even raise them, because these states are less likely to become welfare havens.

Time period. Time-period variables were included to control for the effects of changes in benefit levels occurring nationally. As discussed in chapter 1, in each period the level of benefits declined in comparison with that of the preceding period. This national decline common to all the states needs to be isolated in the analysis in order to detect and explain relative changes in benefit levels among the states.

---

power of the index and was excluded from the model. The results are consistent with Plotnick and Winters, "A Politico-Economic Theory."

43. John H. Fenton, *Midwest Politics* (Holt, Rinehart and Winston, 1966); and Ira Sharkansky, "The Utility of Elazar's Political Culture: A Research Note," *Polity,* vol. 2 (Fall 1969) pp. 66–83.

FIGURE 3-1. A Model of the Factors Determining Changes
in Poverty Rates

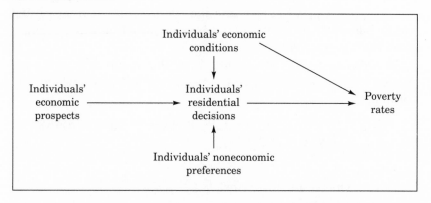

Determinants of Poverty Rates

A model representing the variables that determine changes in
the location of the poor (and thus a state's poverty rate) is presented
in figure 3-1. Economic factors in a state affect both an individual's
likelihood of being in poverty and the individual's residential choice.
Any decision to move is also affected by perceptions of prospects
elsewhere as well as by other preferences we are unable to measure
directly. The sum of these economic effects and residential choices
determines the change in state poverty rates.

Economic conditions have both short-term and longer-term effects
on poverty rates. At any given moment, economic conditions almost
immediately affect a state's poverty rate by influencing the income
of individuals living within the state. The better the job opportunities, the higher the wage levels, and the lower the unemployment
rate, the lower the state's poverty rate. But over time these same
economic conditions may affect the distribution of poverty in quite
the opposite direction by influencing residential decisions. Consider
the following example: If wages within a state rise relative to those
in other states, the immediate economic effect could be to lower
that state's poverty rate as current residents become better off. But
over time these higher wages (relative to other states') may influence
poor people's residential decisions: the poor within the state are

more likely to stay because they know earning opportunities are less elsewhere, while the poor in other states could be induced by these higher wages to move into the state. All other things being equal, higher wages may eventually (and quite ironically) increase the state's poverty rate.

In order to take into account both short-term and long-term factors, we estimated changes in state poverty rates by the following formula:

$$(2) \quad \Delta P_{it} = b_0 + b_1 (B_{ij} \Delta B_{it}) + b_2 W_{ij} + b_3 \Delta E_{it} + b_4 \Delta I_{it} + b_5 \Delta N_{it}$$
$$+ b_6 P_{2it} + b_7 P_{3it} + e_{it},$$

where

ΔP = change in poverty levels;

B = welfare benefit levels;

W = wage levels at beginning of time period;

ΔE = change in number employed;

ΔI = change in per capita income;

ΔN = change in population;

$b_0 \ldots _7$ = coefficients.

Economic conditions. Change in the number employed ($\triangle E$) and change in per capita income ($\triangle I$) measure the effect of short-term economic influences on poverty rates. We hypothesized that as employment opportunities and per capita income increased, the immediate effect would be a decline in the poverty rate.[44] Wage levels at the beginning of the time period (W) were the indicator used to measure longer-term economic influences on the poverty rate. We hypothesized that wage rates influence poverty rates over the longer term by affecting residential choice; if a state's wages are high, poorer citizens will be both retained and attracted into the state at a rate higher than the nonpoor, increasing its poverty

44. Many economists believe that measures of the numbers employed are better indicators of economic opportunities than the more conventional unemployment rate. In other studies unemployment has proven to be an insignificant predictor of migration flows: Gary S. Fields, "Labor Force Migration, Unemployment and Job Turnover," *Review of Economics and Statistics,* vol. 58 (November 1976), pp. 407–15. Our unreported results were consistent with these findings.

rate over time.[45] In other words, we assume that the poor are more likely to move in response to changes in economic opportunities.[46] Note that these hypotheses predict that the coefficients for economic change and level variables will have different signs.[47]

Change in population. It is very difficult to identify a short list of variables indicating noneconomic reasons for residential choices that vary cross-sectionally and over time. To simplify matters, the change in the size of a state's population was included as a proxy for all the unmeasured variables—such as climate or quality of life—that may systematically influence migration patterns.[48] We hypothesized that, controlling for economic change and other factors, the states experiencing greater population growth would also have growing rates of poverty as people with low income, having lower opportunity costs, would be more likely to move to more attractive areas.

Welfare benefits. Welfare benefits are an economic signal like

45. Most previous studies of welfare-induced migration have not discussed the theoretical differences between change and level variables or examined empirically the effects of each and their interaction. However, the topic has provoked at least one academic exchange (see appendix A: Kumar, "More on Nonwhite Migration"; and Cebula, "Nonwhite Migration").

46. L. E. Gallaway, R. F. Gilbert and P. E. Smith, "The Economics of Labor Mobility: An Empirical Analysis," *Western Economic Journal,* vol. 5 (June 1967), pp. 211–23; and Michael J. Greenwood, "The Economics of Labor Mobility: An Empirical Analysis: Comment," *Western Economic Journal,* vol. 6 (June 1968), pp. 243–44.

47. Initially we included in our analysis seven economic variables: change in per capita income, change in wages, change in unemployment rate, change in number of jobs, per capita income, wage levels, and unemployment rate. Preliminary analysis revealed that only the three of these variables retained in the final analysis consistently had coefficients that were significant. We nonetheless interpret these three variables as proxies for a broader range of economic conditions, not discrete economic determinants of poverty rates whose specifically measured effects should be given great policy significance. For example, wage levels and income levels were each positively and significantly associated with increases in poverty rates when the other was omitted from the analysis, but neither remained significant when both were included. Of the two, we selected wage levels for the final equations because the overall explanatory power of the equation was larger when it was included instead of per capita income. However, the substantive interpretation—better economic prospects disproportionately attract the poor—remains the same regardless of the variable included.

48. The increased availability of air conditioners, for example, might have increased the likelihood that people move to Florida and Arizona to enjoy more sun.

any other. Although most people pay welfare policy little mind when considering whether to move, it is possible that those in poverty will be aware of and influenced by the welfare benefits different states offer. One need not think that welfare benefits are the *only* reason that the poor migrate to recognize that those in poverty, like anyone else, are generally mindful of the economic prospects they face in various areas. States offering relatively high benefits are likely to have some attraction for those on society's economic margin.

Since welfare benefit levels were hypothesized to have long-term effects on poverty rates, higher benefit levels were expected to attract and retain low-income residents in the same way higher wage rates did. We also hypothesized that increases in the benefit levels would have a smaller but still positive immediate effect on changes in the poverty rate. Furthermore, we hypothesized that benefit levels at the end of the period (equivalent to the interactive effect between the other two poverty variables) would affect poverty rates, with migration depending on expectations of the benefit levels at the end of the period. To examine this possibility, we estimated the effect of welfare benefits two different ways. In the first, we entered into the equation both initial benefit levels and changes in benefits during the period, while in the second we used only the expectations term.[49] Although the results from the first equation supported our hypotheses (see appendix C), the estimation using only the expectations term produced larger and more significant coefficients.

National trends. Since our analysis combines data from three successive time periods, it is important to control for changes in poverty rates occurring nationally from one time period to the next. Over the fifteen-year period under investigation, national changes in poverty rates were substantial.[50] The average state poverty rate

49. Because of a very high degree of multicollinearity, entering all three terms in one equation would produce unreliable results. Michael S. Lewis-Beck discusses the use of interactive terms in *Applied Regression: An Introduction* (Beverly Hills: Sage Publications, 1980), pp. 54–56.

50. The increases in poverty after 1975 are due in part to the decline in hourly earnings among workers and in part to the increase in female-headed households. James P. Smith, "Poverty and the Family," in Gary D. Sandefur and Marta Tienda,

fell from 14.6 percent in 1969 to 11.8 percent in 1975 before rising to 13.5 percent in 1980 and 14.2 percent in 1985. The inclusion of the time-period variables in the analysis enables us to isolate these changes from the changes in the interstate variation in poverty rates that are the focus of our analysis.

All monetary data reported here are calculated in constant dollars, using 1985 as the base year.[51]

Determinants of Poverty Rates and Welfare Benefits

The results from four separate regressions for both the poverty and benefits equations are presented in tables 3-1 and 3-2. The first two columns in each table include coefficients and summary statistics from the recursive equations using an ordinary least squares estimation. The third and fourth columns are from the simultaneous equations and are estimated by the two-stage least squares technique. Columns 1 and 3 are estimations from the raw data, while in columns 2 and 4 the data have been converted into logarithms. The results from all estimations are similar, but our interpretation will rely primarily on the simultaneous equations using the transformed data (column 4).[52] Because the interpretation of the coeffi-

---

eds., *Divided Opportunities: Minorities, Poverty, and Social Policy* (New York: Plenum Press, 1988), pp. 141–72. The increases are also due in part to a statistical fluke, the result of changes in the consumer price index in the 1970s that exceeded real changes in the actual cost of living during this period. Although the Department of Labor corrected the CPI in 1979, it did not make its corrections retroactive, and, as a result, any measure tied to the CPI, as is the poverty index, has been artificially increased. John C. Weicher, "Mismeasuring Poverty and Progress," American Enterprise Institute for Public Policy Research, December 1986. Since we are controlling for national trends, these issues are not addressed in this analysis.

51. The use of constant rather than current dollars does not affect the size of the coefficients in the equation, though it does affect the sign on the time-period variables.

52. Preference for logged or unlogged data depends on expectations about marginal relationships, precision of the coefficients, and overall goodness of fit for the model (Hanushek and Jackson, *Statistical Methods,* pp. 100–01). There is no reason to believe that there is a linear relationship between the variables; the marginal relationships from the logged equations are quite consistent with theoretical expectations. The transformed data appear to yield superior estimates by the last two criteria: they provide more precise estimates (judging by the size of the *t*-statistics) and smaller standard errors for the entire model. Two-stage least squares

TABLE 3-1. Explaining Changes in Poverty[a]

| | Recursive model | | Simultaneous model (two-stage) | |
| | Unlogged | Logged | Unlogged | Logged |
Predictor	(1)	(2)	(3)	(4)
$B\Delta B$ (benefits)	0.20	0.12*	0.27*	0.17†
	(1.4)	(1.7)	(1.7)	(2.2)
ΔI (income)	−0.46	−0.50*	−0.53*	−0.58†
	(1.6)	(1.8)	(1.8)	(2.0)
ΔE (employment)	−0.71*	−0.79†	−0.64*	−0.72*
	(1.9)	(2.2)	(1.7)	(1.9)
W (wages)	0.36‡	0.28‡	0.34‡	0.26‡
	(3.0)	(2.9)	(2.8)	(2.6)
ΔN (population)	0.51	0.57	0.42	0.48*
	(1.2)	(1.4)	(0.9)	(1.7)
P_2 (period 2)	0.36‡	0.36‡	0.36‡	0.36‡
	(8.9)	(10.0)	(8.7)	(10.0)
P_3 (period 3)	0.22‡	0.23‡	0.23‡	0.24‡
	(4.6)	(5.3)	(4.7)	(5.6)
Intercept	1.14‡	−0.28*	1.20‡	−0.37†
	(2.8)	(1.9)	(2.9)	(2.3)
Summary statistics				
R^2	0.54	0.60	0.55	0.60
Standard error[b]	0.16	0.16	0.16	0.16
F-statistic	22.91	28.52	23.09	29.01
N	143	143	142	142

* Significant at the 10 percent level.
† Significant at the 5 percent level.
‡ Significant at the 1 percent level.
a. Numbers in parentheses are t-statistics.
b. To make direct cross-equation goodness-of-fit comparisons possible, the standard error for the logged equations was recalculated by taking the antilog of the predicted values and then calculating the squared difference between the actual and predicted values. This is the standard error reported here.

cients in the logged equations is complex (they show changes in proportional rates of change between the independent and dependent variables), we will describe the results in terms of the underlying variables. To make clear the effect of the coefficients on the variables within a likely range, we present in table 3-3 the amount benefit

estimation provides superior (consistent) estimates over ordinary least squares in nonrecursive equations.

TABLE 3-2. Explaining Changes in Cash and Food Stamp Benefits[a]

Predictor	Recursive model		Simultaneous model (two-stage)	
	Unlogged	Logged	Unlogged	Logged
	(1)	(2)	(3)	(4)
$P\Delta P$ (poverty)	−0.53‡	−0.08‡	−0.41†	−0.08‡
	(3.0)	(3.0)	(2.2)	(2.8)
T (tax effort)	0.18‡	0.21‡	0.17‡	0.20‡
	(4.4)	(4.8)	(4.2)	(4.6)
C (tax capacity)	0.05	0.10†	0.06*	0.09†
	(1.5)	(2.3)	(1.7)	(2.2)
PI (politics)	0.18†	0.02†	0.18†	0.02†
	(2.3)	(2.3)	(2.3)	(2.2)
B (benefits)	−0.53‡	−0.39‡	−0.50‡	−0.40‡
	(8.4)	(8.6)	(8.0)	(8.5)
P_2 (period 2)	−0.11‡	−0.12‡	−0.11‡	−0.11‡
	(8.2)	(8.2)	(7.9)	(7.9)
P_3 (period 3)	−0.10‡	−0.10‡	−0.09‡	−0.10‡
	(6.6)	(6.6)	(6.1)	(6.3)
Intercept	1.16‡	0.62‡	1.12‡	0.60‡
	(15.7)	(6.2)	(15.2)	(5.9)
Summary statistics				
R^2	0.53	0.55	0.52	0.54
Standard error[b]	0.06	0.06	0.06	0.06
F-statistic	22.7	24.0	20.8	22.8
N	146	146	142	142

* Significant at the 10 percent level.
† Significant at the 5 percent level.
‡ Significant at the 1 percent level.
a. Numbers in parentheses are t-statistics.
b. See note b, table 3-1.

levels would change as each causal factor shifts from a low level to a high level.[53] In table 3-4 we present the same information for changes in poverty levels.

The results indicate that policymakers take into account the poverty rate–and the interstate migration of the poor—when estab-

53. A high level is one standard deviation above the mean; a low level is one standard deviation below it.

TABLE 3-3. Estimated Effects on Benefit Levels of Shifts in
Independent Variables
Dollars

Independent variable	Effect on annual benefit levels of shift in independent variables from low to high[a]
Poverty rate[b]	−384
Initial benefit level[c]	−1,212
Tax effort[d]	516
Tax capacity[e]	240
Political competition[f]	180

a. The estimations were made by setting to zero the effects of the mean values of all explanatory variables on benefits and then estimating the effect of a change from one standard deviation below the mean to one standard deviation above the mean for each explanatory variable.
b. High = 17.5 percent; low = 9 percent.
c. High = $801; low = $521 (monthly payments).
d. High = 1.12; low = 0.79 (see appendix B).
e. High = 1.17; low = 0.81 (see appendix B).
f. High = 0.24; low = 0.07 (see appendix B).

lishing welfare policy. If poverty levels in a state are high instead of low, annual welfare benefits for a four-person family fall by $384 (see table 3-3).

This effect of poverty on welfare policy can be interpreted in two different ways. One possibility is that state policymakers have a more or less fixed budget for welfare expenditure. As the number of recipients increases, the allocation per recipient declines. Our estimates (not presented here) suggest that in the average state an increase of one standard deviation in the poverty rate would raise its welfare costs by $44 million a year by adding new recipients to the rolls. The state would offset this cost by reducing welfare benefits by an amount that saves the state $13 million. Since the savings that come from benefit reductions are less than one-third the increased costs of assisting new recipients, the budget is clearly not on automatic pilot, equilibrating benefits with every change in the welfare rolls.[54] Also, if it were simply a matter of keeping the welfare budget constant, then welfare policies should be more sensitive to changes in the number of welfare recipients than to

54. Texas has a constitutional amendment prohibiting it from spending more than 1 percent of state revenues on welfare, but it is the only state with such a constitutionally fixed limit.

TABLE 3-4. Estimated Effects on Poverty Levels of Shifts in
Independent Variables
Percent

Independent variable	Effect on poverty level of shift in independent variables from low to high[a]
Monthly welfare benefits[b]	0.9
Change in per capita income[c]	−1.0
Hourly wages[d]	1.0
Change in employment[e]	−1.7
Change in population size[f]	0.8

a. The estimations were made by setting to zero the effects of the mean values of all explanatory variables on the poverty level and then estimating the effect of a change from one standard deviation below the mean to one standard deviation above the mean for each explanatory variable.
b. High = $722; low = $476.
c. High = 15.5 percent; low = 0.1 percent.
d. High = $10.52; low = $7.94.
e. High = 23.9 percent; low = 0.3 percent.
f. High = 13.1 percent; low = 0.0 percent.

changes in the poverty rates. As the number of recipients increases, the level of support should drop accordingly. But the connection between changes in the number of welfare recipients and welfare policies proved to be insignificant (see appendix C).

That states seemed more sensitive to the overall size of the poor population than to changes in the number of welfare recipients raises a second possibility: that changes in the size of the poor population are visible to the general public and thus politically salient. As the number of poor increases, so do the demands on a variety of social service delivery systems, including the schools, hospitals, fire departments, and the police. Politicians, interest groups, and the news media may raise questions concerning where poor people are coming from and what factors are bringing them to the state. The exact mechanisms connecting these events to public policy probably vary from state to state, but they seem to result from broader forces than mere budgetary considerations.

Such reductions in welfare benefits are understandable, given the effect of benefit levels on the location of the poor. A state offering high welfare benefits will have a poverty rate 0.9 percent higher than a state providing low benefits (see table 3-4). These differences in poverty rates are most probably due to migration rather than to welfare-induced changes in labor force participation rates or household formation. This inference is supported by the finding that welfare benefits have much the same effect on changes in the percentage of a state's population that is black as they do on poverty rates (see appendix C). Since changes in the racial composition of a state's population (compared with that in other states) are almost certainly a function of net migration rates, it is very likely that the similar welfare-induced changes in poverty rates are also a function of migration.

Benefit levels and wages have almost identical effects on poverty rates. A state with a high hourly wage has a poverty rate 1.0 percent higher than a state with low wages. Rapid population growth also contributes to increases in poverty: a state having high population growth over a five-year period will have a poverty rate 0.8 percent higher than a state with low population growth.

While states with high welfare benefits, high wage rates, and population growth experience quite similar increases in their poverty rates, states with rapidly growing economies enjoy shrinking poverty rates. Rising per capita income depresses poverty: a state with high per capita income growth over five years will experience a 1 percent greater reduction in its poverty rate than a state with low income growth. More important, a large increase in employment over five years reduces poverty 1.7 percent more than a small increase. As might be expected in a society in which income is not equally distributed, growth in the number of jobs reduces poverty faster than growth in per capita income. Indeed, changes in employment rates affect poverty levels substantially more than any other single variable.

Although none of these factors individually has a dramatic effect on the distribution of poverty in the United States, they are not insignificant. For an average-sized state, an increase in the poverty rate of 1 percent adds about 55,000 to the rolls of the poor. And, except for changes in employment, welfare benefits have about as strong an effect on the location of the poor as any of the other variables.

Benefit levels are the only identifiable factor influencing poverty rates that state policymakers directly control, and the evidence is considerable that state politicians take into account the effect of increases in poverty on the state's economy. Not only do states with rising poverty reduce their benefits, but states with relatively high benefits—fearful, we suspect, of becoming welfare havens—cut them. A state with a high welfare guarantee at the beginning of our five-year period would, all else being equal, slash its annual benefits by $1,212 by the period's end (see table 3-3).

This may be understood as a powerful convergence factor that shapes policy outcomes. If a state's benefits are higher than those of its peers, pressures increase on policymakers to adjust their benefits downward. Given these competitive pressures from other states, one might expect that policies among the states would eventually converge to a single national standard, the result of mutual policy adjustment. Several things must be understood about this convergence, however. First, it does not happen all that quickly. In a computer simulation in which initial benefit levels were the only explanatory variable and monthly benefits were spread from a low of $476 to a high of $722 (one standard deviation above and below the mean for our data set), after four periods (twenty years) the most generous state had lowered its benefits to $624 and the least generous had raised its to $570. Second, the convergence can occur around a steadily falling average. The point at which benefits converge depends on how the average state reacts. If a state offering the average level of welfare does not cut its benefits, then benefit levels will converge at approximately this average. But if states at the average perceive themselves as still too generous and cut their benefits, the average benefit level will spiral downward.[55] This in fact appears to have happened, as welfare benefits have steadily declined since 1970.

The pressures toward convergence are also offset by opposing political and economic factors. The most important of these seems to be the political culture of the state, as measured by a state's willingness to tax itself. A state with a high tax effort increases its

55. This is a matter of changing the intercept term. In our simulations in which the average state does not cut its benefits, its intercept (for the logged estimation) is calculated as: intercept $= 1/(B)^{-0.40}$. B = average benefits and -0.40 is the benefits coefficient from our empirical estimations (table 3-2). Reducing the size of the intercept means that the average state will cut its benefits. To show this we used the intercept: intercept $= 0.9/(B)^{-0.40}$. In this case the average benefit level in our simulation dropped from $599 a month to $486 after four periods.

benefits by $516 a year more than a state with a low tax effort (see table 3-3). Greater political competitiveness and state wealth also contribute to rising benefits: a highly competitive state is predicted to increase benefits by $180 a year more than one with little political competition, and a state with high tax capacity by $240 a year more than a state with low tax capacity.

These results suggest that state policymakers take into account multiple signals in determining welfare benefit guarantees. States that are more prosperous, more politically competitive, and culturally more disposed toward redistribution are likely to increase welfare benefits over time and in comparison with other states. But high and increasing poverty levels lead to cuts in welfare. High benefit levels also expose states to welfare-induced migration of the poor. During the 1970s and 1980s the conditions that promote higher benefits were outweighed by forces that prompted benefit cuts.

How characteristic of these overall patterns were the trends in poverty rates and benefit levels in Wisconsin? The similarities have been evident throughout the analysis, but there are some differences worth noting. Perhaps the most significant was the rate of increase in poverty. The model estimated this to be 17 percent for Wisconsin between 1980 and 1985, but poverty actually increased by 36 percent. No wonder Wisconsin politicians were especially alarmed at the changes that were occurring. Also, the real decline in Wisconsin welfare benefits was only $40 during these same years, less than half the $90 decline the model predicted. Perhaps our numerical indicators did not capture certain elements in Wisconsin's political culture and competitive politics that made the state especially resistant to demands for welfare cuts. Or perhaps the model explains why this issue exploded so virulently in Wisconsin politics in 1986. Since the policymaking system had not adjusted in the usual manner over the previous five years, the context was ripe for heated political controversy.

Conclusions

The research that we have reported is consistent with theoretical analyses showing that state and local governments in a federal system will tend to provide less income redistribution than a national government would. Each state government acts as if it prefers that welfare services should be provided by other governments and fears that its state will become attractive to poor people if it provides generous benefits.

State redistributive policies are less generous than a national policy in part because low-income people are sensitive to interstate differences in welfare policy. This does not mean that large numbers of poor people rush from one state to another with every modest adjustment in state benefit levels. But the data do suggest that over time, as people make major decisions about whether they should move or remain where they are, they take into account the level of welfare a state provides and the extent to which that level is increasing. The poor do this roughly to the same extent that they respond to differences in wage opportunities in other states.

It may be argued that welfare policy should vary from one part of the country to another so that people with differing ideas about the desirable level of redistribution can live in a state whose practices conform to their own beliefs. There is some evidence in our data to support this argument. In states with a liberal political culture, as measured by a state's tax effort, welfare benefits tend to increase relative to other states'. Welfare benefits also increase in states that have higher levels of political competition and electoral participation. But if these findings provide some support for this argument, other findings give as much or more support to the counterargument that welfare benefits for the poor should not depend on the accidents of a state's wealth, as measured, for example, by its tax capacity or the size of its low-income population.

Welfare policy in the United States has already begun to take these economic realities and equitable considerations into account. As the nation's economy has become increasingly integrated during the postwar period, the fiscal responsibility for welfare has steadily shifted to the national government. In 1940 the federal government paid for only 38 percent of the cost of the cash maintenance program. By 1985 the federal share had increased to 77 percent, taking food stamp contributions into account. In the next chapter we look more carefully at these evolutionary developments in U.S. welfare policy.

Chapter 4

The Evolution of Welfare Policy

T HE EVOLUTION of social policy in the United States has been influenced by the interplay of four political and governmental factors. First and foremost, the distribution of political power among competing political and social interests provides the context within which debates over welfare policy take place. A coalition of reform-minded moderates and liberals has generally been the driving force behind the gradual expansion and centralization of welfare policy throughout the twentieth century. Opposition has typically come from conservatives opposed to nationally controlled welfare policies, southerners who wish to safeguard state and regional autonomy, and, on occasion, from liberals worried that institutional change would adversely affect the immediate interests of their supporters.

Second, it has often been the welfare policy specialists who have defined the problem, assembled the evidence, devised the seemingly viable solutions, convinced the politicians of the need for change, and gained the publicity necessary to build a national movement. Reform has often come from above, not below. A small number of committed, middle-class professionals, not a broad base of mobilized supporters, have generally provided the political impetus for reform.[1]

1. Hugh Heclo, *A Government of Strangers: Executive Politics in Washington* (Brookings, 1977); Martha Derthick, *Policymaking for Social Security* (Brookings, 1979); Daniel P. Moynihan, *Maximum Feasible Misunderstanding: Community Action in the War on Poverty* (Free Press, 1969); and Lawrence M. Friedman, "The Social and Political Context of the War on Poverty: An Overview," in Robert H. Haveman, ed., *A Decade of Federal Antipoverty Programs: Achievements, Failures and Lessons* (Academic Press, 1977), pp. 21–47. This view is also drawn upon in Daniel P.

Third, these professional efforts have been more effective when the nation has been perceived to be in the midst of a major social or political crisis. Some have argued, in fact, that only when the poor threaten the stability of the political order do they acquire the power necessary to win significant reforms. Since the poor lack the political resources that most interest groups rely upon to shape legislation, they must rely on the one resource they uniquely have: they can afford social disruption. As Kris Kristofferson put it so well, "Freedom's just another word for nothin' left to lose."[2] Most of the time, of course, the poor do not challenge the stability of the social system, but from time to time they protest, demonstrate, riot, or otherwise disrupt the normal functioning of social institutions. Under these circumstances, political leaders pay attention to the recommendations of policy analysts they typically ignore. And once these policy recommendations have been turned into operating welfare state programs, these programs have "themselves created or nurtured the organized political forces that defend the welfare state."[3]

Fourth, these group conflicts and professional recommendations take place in a governmental structure that constrains policy choice. Policymaking in the United States is marked by the fragmentation of power between the state and federal governments (federalism) and among Congress, the president, and the courts (separation of powers). As a result of these divisions, the administrative structure necessary to execute nationally determined welfare policies is present in only nascent form. State agencies resist the development of a national competitor, and the constitutional status of national administrative structures was subject to skeptical judicial scrutiny

---

Moynihan, *The Politics of a Guaranteed Income: The Nixon Administration and the Family Assistance Plan* (Random House, 1973), but in this volume the role of professionals is subordinated to the pattern of group conflict.

2. "Me and Bobby McGee," by Kris Kristofferson and Fred L. Foster. © 1969 TEMI Combine Inc. All rights controlled by Combine Music Corp. and admininstered by EMI Blackwood Music Inc. All rights reserved. International copyright secured. Used by permission.

3. Frances Fox Piven and Richard A. Cloward, *The New Class War: Reagan's Attack on the Welfare State and Its Consequences,* rev. ed. (Pantheon, 1985), p. 184. Also see an earlier version of their argument in Frances Fox Piven and Richard A. Cloward, *Regulating the Poor: The Functions of Public Welfare* (Pantheon, 1971).

until the postwar years. As a result, even proponents of social reform have traditionally been leery of national administrative structures and have attempted whenever possible to use state and local agencies to carry out national policy. Important substantive objectives have been sacrificed in order to put into place a politically acceptable administrative organization. The final key to understanding welfare policy in the United States is thus the institutional terrain on which groups compete.[4]

In short, a particular configuration of interests, policy analyses, social conflicts, and institutional structures has shaped the drive for expanding and centralizing welfare policy in the United States. A closer examination of how these forces have shaped welfare policy in the past will help illuminate the possibilities for change.

Mothers' Pensions

The general shape that the politics of welfare would take throughout the twentieth century was evident from its very beginning. First, the leadership came not from the poor and the dependent themselves but from middle-class groups concerned about their well-being. The campaign for assistance to needy families was inaugurated by reform-minded, middle-class groups that formed an integral part of the Progressive movement. Many of their leaders felt that some kind of assistance for fatherless families was a necessary part of the campaign to eliminate child labor and institute compulsory education. Second, the design of the welfare assistance program was shaped by the institutional realities of the time. In those early days there was no question but that such assistance would be state-financed and -administered. Not only were there doubts about the constitutional capacity of the federal government to provide welfare, but there was widespread suspicion that any nationally administered program would fall prey to the partisanship and corruption that

4. Margaret Weir, Ann Shola Orloff, and Theda Skocpol, eds., *The Politics of Social Policy in the United States* (Princeton University Press, 1988); Stephen Skowronek, *Building a New American State: The Expansion of National Administrative Capacities, 1877–1920* (Cambridge University Press, 1982); and Christopher Leman, *The Collapse of Welfare Reform: Political Institutions, Policy, and the Poor in Canada and the United States* (MIT Press, 1980).

had marked the federal system of pensions distributed to Civil War veterans and their families.

The nature of the opposition also presaged the conflicts that would follow in the decades to come. Mothers' pension laws, the name given to the earliest version of welfare assistance, encountered strong resistance from rural, southern, and conservative interests. Even something like the later liberal opposition to welfare reform was evident in these early years. Private charities, suspicious of a shift in institutional power, opposed the public assumption of welfare responsibility.

The impetus for mothers' pensions came from a White House Conference on the Care of Dependent Children that President Theodore Roosevelt had called into being in 1909. Even at the birth of the pension idea, the question of a federal role was soon put to rest as Roosevelt quickly removed himself, his administration, and the federal government from any responsibility for the problems of dependent children. While he eagerly affirmed his commitment to their care—"The goal toward which we should strive is to help . . . [the single] mother, so that she can keep her own home and keep the child in it"—he was equally eager to hand the responsibility for providing such care over to others—"How the relief shall come, public, private, or by a mixture of both, in what way, you are competent to say and I am not."[5] The conference itself did not even recommend state assistance to the needy, but said that widows should be supported by private sources. But the precise nature of the conference's recommendations seems to have been less important than the fact that it focused public attention on the problem of fatherless homes. The inadequacy of private sources of support became immediately evident, especially in the Midwest and West, where private charities were at best weak and fragile institutions. Within two years of the conference, mothers' pension laws were enacted in Illinois and Missouri, a decade later forty states had

5. Mark H. Leff, quoted in John Clayton Drew, "Child Labor and Child Welfare: The Origins and Uneven Development of the American Welfare State," Ph.D. dissertation, Cornell University, 1987, p. 137. Our discussion of the mothers' pension movement is drawn from Drew's comprehensive study of the origins and spread of this welfare policy innovation.

enacted similar laws, and by 1931 only Georgia and South Carolina had not adopted such legislation.

The campaign for mothers' pensions derived directly from the child labor movement. The advocates of laws regarding child labor and compulsory education had for years argued that children should not be working in sweatshops but should be learning in school. Opponents of this legislation argued that the children in fatherless families needed to work in order to supplement the inadequate incomes of their mothers: taking these children out of the factory would drive the family into the poorhouse. The initial reaction of the advocates of child labor laws was to deny the dependence of families on child labor; in the words of one leader, "Only a small proportion of [working] children could be the children of widows; [and] . . . only a small proportion of those widows were dependent upon the earnings of their children."[6] But many female-headed families could ill afford to lose the income from a child's earnings, however small. The more thoughtful of the juvenile court judges who had the responsibility for enforcing child labor laws recognized the "inconsistency" in many instances of "demanding that a child obey these [child-labor] laws and requiring the family to stay self-sufficient."[7] Supporters of child labor laws such as Jane Addams in Chicago and the Child Labor Committee in New York City tried to compensate these families by creating private "scholarships" for the children of widows who remained in school.[8] But private funds soon proved inadequate to meet the need, and after the White House conference reformers looked to public sources for support.

Although the campaign for mothers' pensions spread like wildfire in midwestern and western states between 1911 and 1913, the program encountered stronger resistance in other parts of the country. In the South, opposition came from farmers and textile companies still dependent on inexpensive labor. Opposition in the East came not so much from economic and other conservative

6. Homer Folks, quoted in Drew, "Child Labor and Child Welfare," p. 99. The remarks are Folks's confession of the position his allies in the child labor movement had taken before they realized the need for mothers' pensions.

7. Drew, "Child Labor and Child Welfare," p. 140.

8. Drew, "Child Labor and Child Welfare," pp. 101–16.

interests as from groups that supposedly had the interests of the poor foremost in mind. In an ironic precursor of the liberal opposition to welfare reforms in the 1970s, mothers' pensions were opposed by the Charity Organizing Society, a group representing orphanages and charity groups that had assumed the primary responsibility for the care of fatherless children. The threat posed by mothers' pensions to these organizations was readily apparent. As the secretary of the Baltimore society observed, "No private fund for relief can successfully compete very long with a public fund, whether the latter is adequate or not. Inevitably the sources of private charitable relief dry up."[9] But the argument they made in opposition to mothers' pensions went beyond self-interest. Public aid, they pointed out, invited politics and corruption. As New York reform Mayor Seth Low had discovered about other public relief programs, "The friends of politicians received help whether needy or not, and so the system was perpetuated."[10]

Even after this opposition had been defeated and mothers' pension laws enacted in all but two states, the pensions typically had many limitations. Most states had residency requirements that denied aid to newcomers, no matter how needy. The programs also served only the limited set of poor families regarded as deserving. A scant 4 percent of the families receiving benefits were nonwhite. Only 7 percent of the families receiving mothers' pensions had a father who was absent due to divorce or desertion.

Benefits varied widely among the states. The average monthly grant was as high as $69 in Massachusetts and as low as $4 in Arkansas.[11] Furthermore, although the pensions were authorized by state laws, the actual costs were usually borne by county governments. Consequently, over half the counties in the United States chose not to implement the program.[12] Among counties that did participate, benefit levels varied widely—even within states. In

9. Quoted in Drew, "Child Labor and Child Welfare," p. 169.
10. Blanche Coll, quoted in Drew, "Child Labor and Child Welfare," p. 168.
11. Drew, "Child Labor and Child Welfare," p. 149.
12. In 1934, for example, counties contributed $37 million to the program while states contributed only $6 million. *Economic Security Act,* Hearings before the House Committee on Ways and Means, 74 Cong. 1 sess. (Government Printing Office, 1935), p. 158.

Illinois, for example, annual benefits per child ranged from $19 to $238, a range that was not unusual.

Establishing a Federal Welfare System

The middle-class reformers who campaigned for mothers' pensions in the first two decades of the century were also the mainstay of support for the single most important restructuring of mothers' pensions laws, which took place as part of the social security legislation promulgated in 1935. But this time reformers were acting in the midst of a national economic and political crisis that enabled them to win the support of both Democratic and Republican party leaders for an expansion and centralization of welfare policy that had seemed out of the question in less threatening times. Signs of conservative opposition still remained, but they were able only to contain, not stop, the forces of reform. The extent of the reform was also limited by the institutional structure that had developed as part of the mothers' pension laws. Once the country had committed itself to a state-based system of welfare assistance, it was not easy to transform it into a nationally administered program.

The spark that ignited the demand for more centralized direction of public assistance programs was financial. The locally funded mothers' pension programs were caught in a fiscal crisis created by the Depression, which increased demands for assistance at the very time it reduced the revenues to fund it. The first response to this problem during Franklin Roosevelt's remarkable One Hundred Days was to create the Federal Emergency Relief Administration (FERA), which temporarily relieved states and localities of many of their responsibilities for the destitute.

To develop a longer-term solution to welfare issues highlighted by the Depression, Roosevelt appointed in 1934 a high-level inter-agency committee, the Committee on Economic Security (CES), to develop comprehensive legislation to enhance "the security of the men, women, and children of the Nation against certain hazards and vicissitudes of life."[13] The administrative arrangements for

13. "Message from the President," in *Economic Security Act,* Hearings, p. 13. The CES consisted of the secretary of labor as chair, the FERA administrator, the

economic security proposed by the CES were shaped as much by the country's governmental structure as by the needs of the national economy. Several members of the CES (most particularly, Edwin Witte, the University of Wisconsin economist who became the committee's executive director) had worked with state programs and were reluctant to see state initiatives totally subordinated to federal control. The CES was also worried about constitutional issues; given the state of legal doctrine and the makeup of the Supreme Court, it was not clear that the federal government would be granted the authority to establish national social welfare programs. And they were generally uncertain of the administrative capacities of the federal government. Committee members worried greatly that brand-new agencies would have neither the expertise nor the wisdom necessary to make key administrative decisions.

Yet the CES and its advisers also recognized that the problem of economic security could not be addressed without significantly increasing federal authority. By the 1930s the national economy was well integrated, and capital and labor were becoming increasingly mobile. The CES realized that security in a nationally integrated economy could be achieved only through national programs that did not unduly help or hinder businesses or workers on the basis of location.

Searching for a compromise that would balance these competing political and economic considerations, the committee divided the population into categories, ceding federal authority only where a nationally uniform program seemed absolutely necessary:

The measures we suggest all seek to segregate clearly distinguishable large groups among those now on relief or on the verge

---

attorney general and the secretaries of Treasury and Agriculture. The CES was aided by a number of working groups with responsibility for particular issues. Summaries of the CES's work can be found in Edwin E. Witte, *The Development of the Social Security Act: A Memorandum on the History of the Committee on Economic Security and Drafting and Legislative History of the Social Security Act* (University of Wisconsin Press, 1962); and Committee on Economic Security, *Social Security in America: The Factual Background of the Social Security Act as Summarized from Staff Reports to the Committee on Economic Security,* Social Security Board Pub. 20 (GPO, 1937). As used in the text, *CES* will refer to the committee, its staff, and the associated working groups.

of relief and to apply such differentiated treatment to each group as will give it the greatest practical degree of economic security. . . . The residual relief problem will . . . [then diminish] . . . to a point where it will be possible to return primary responsibility for the care of people who cannot work to the state and local governments.[14]

The key to distinguishing between national and state responsibilities was the closeness of the connection between the category of individuals and the functional requirements of the national economy. The most clear-cut case for federal control was retirement benefits for lifelong workers. The CES recommended an almost completely federally funded and administered old-age insurance program because of the "actuarial soundness of distributing the risk broadly and the interstate character of the labor market, with its high mobility of workers between states during their long period of contribution."[15] Not only did analysis suggest that a national system of old-age insurance was economically appropriate, but popular sentiment also seemed to make it politically attractive. The Townsendites were demanding large retirement pensions, and this movement was "especially influential in Congress, . . . with local clubs [active] in almost every congressional district."[16] Furthermore, although private pension plans were adamantly opposed to the program, there was no significant opposition from state agencies. Although a number of states had established old-age assistance programs, they were quite small and most were in financial difficulty. Their programs would continue in any case as part of the old-age assistance program that would remain in effect until old-age insurance coverage became universal.[17] Thus the popular program now

14. *Congressional Record,* January 17, 1935, p. 548.

15. Theron F. Schlabach, *Edwin E. Witte: Cautious Reformer* (Madison: State Historical Society of Wisconsin, 1969), p. 117.

16. Ann Shola Orloff, "The Political Origins of America's Belated Welfare State," in Weir, Orloff, and Skocpol, *Politics of Social Policy,* p. 68; she cites Abraham Holtzman, *The Townsend Movement: A Political Study* (New York: Bookman Associates, 1963).

17. For a description of the state programs, see CES, *Social Security in America,* pp. 155–66.

known as social security was established from the beginning as a nationally controlled, nationally funded, uniformly administered federal program.

The committee's thinking on the financing of unemployment compensation was just as unequivocal: a national, uniform payroll tax was necessary to remove the unfair competitive advantage that employers operating in states without a compensation plan would enjoy over employers operating in states that gave such protection to their wage earners. The significance of interstate competition in this area was readily apparent to the CES; Edwin Witte came from Wisconsin, the only state that at the time had an unemployment compensation program. The CES staff explicitly observed that while "many factors accounted for this record of almost complete failure" to enact unemployment compensation laws, "the most important was the fear of the states that passage of an unemployment compensation law would put their employers at a competitive disadvantage with employers in states which had no similar law."[18]

There were other advantages to a national unemployment compensation program, of course. A national system created a broad pool of funds that could be used wherever unemployment existed; thus it could spread out the risks more than could separate programs funded by individual states. A national program could provide uniform protection to workers no matter where they lived. And because workers would be said to have earned this nationally established insurance, identical tax rates "furnished an easy and uniform method of handling the problem of interstate employees."[19]

Yet for all the advantages of a national system of unemployment compensation, the committee left many questions, including the actual benefits workers would receive, to state discretion. There was concern, augmented by the lack of an experienced national administrative structure, that a national system would create a cumbersome bureaucracy. If decisions taken by inexperienced administrators were in error, they would have more serious consequences and wider repercussions than would state-level decisions. Not only did Witte, as one of the originators of the Wisconsin law,

18. CES, *Social Security in America*, pp. 91, 93.
19. CES, *Social Security in America*, p. 93.

want to preserve state discretion, but President Roosevelt, himself a former state governor, also had "decided preferences for state administration of unemployment insurance."[20] Thus it was decided that even though the unemployment compensation tax would be uniform throughout the country, the federal government would "leave wide latitude to the States in other respects" in order to respond to local conditions.[21] Among other advantages, state control would permit compensation levels to vary with differences in local wage levels.

But even though a good deal of state discretion remained, the decision to impose a nationally uniform tax limited competition among the states. A state had little incentive to lower its benefits too much below the levels in other states; this would let the taxes paid by businesses in that state be siphoned off to pay high benefits to workers in other states. As a result, unemployment compensation benefits developed along more uniform lines than did welfare programs that had no uniform funding arrangement (see discussion in chapter 1).

The remaining economic security programs recommended by the CES had less federal direction. The amount of aid given to the blind and the elderly not covered by social security insurance—those known as the "deserving poor" because it was generally accepted that they could not become a regular part of the work force—was to be determined mainly at the discretion of state governments. The federal government, however, for the first time began to help finance these programs. Indeed, Congress even went beyond the recommendation of the CES that the federal government pay 33 percent of the cost of these programs, legislating a 50 percent federal contribution instead.[22]

The general reluctance to override state and local authority was even more evident in the CES's recommendations with respect to the mothers' pensions. Both the Townsend movement and economic considerations had driven the CES to favor national programs for the unemployed and the elderly. Families with dependent children,

20. Witte, *Development of the Social Security Act,* p. 18.
21. *Congressional Record,* January 17, 1935, pp. 545–49, quote on p. 546.
22. The amount of aid was limited by a maximum amount per recipient, however.

however, had no comparable group representing them, and, since they were outside the work force, there was no immediately compelling economic reason to nationalize the program. Almost all states already had a mothers' pension program that supposedly could meet their needs, and federal assistance was necessary only to help sustain these programs. Indeed, some thought it remarkable that Congress approved any program of aid to dependent children (ADC). When Witte wrote down his remembrances of the work of the committee some years later, he observed: "There was little interest in Congress in the aid to dependent children. It is my belief that nothing would have been done on this subject if it had not been included in the report of the Committee on Economic Security."[23]

Although the recollection was probably too self-congratulatory, it does indicate the extent to which this reform depended on the support of a fairly small group of welfare professionals. Witte certainly offered the most influential testimony when he made the case for the Roosevelt administration that "our American civilization has concluded that the best way to make provision for these young families without fathers is to make a long-time provision . . . under which the children can be cared for in their own homes and under their mother's guidance. That is the most humane and efficient way of meeting this problem."[24] The proposal also had the backing of the Children's Bureau, a small but energetic agency within the Department of Labor,[25] and it was endorsed as well by the fledgling social work community: Grace Abbott, a professor of public welfare at the University of Chicago and a member of the CES's advisory group, iterated the practical reasons for aid that had always been given by supporters of mothers' pensions: "The children can be taken care of more cheaply in their own homes by their mothers than they can be taken care of in foster homes or in institutions."[26]

Overtly, the campaign for public assistance for families with

23. Witte, *Development of the Social Security Act,* p. 164.

24. *Economic Security Act,* Hearings, p. 159.

25. Michael B. Katz, *In the Shadow of the Poorhouse: A Social History of Welfare in America* (Basic Books, 1986), p. 237.

26. *Economic Security Act,* Hearings before the Senate Committee on Finance, 74 Cong. 1 sess. (GPO, 1935), p. 1084.

dependent children was nothing more than a group of well-informed professional insiders calling for what they saw as a needed policy innovation. The lack of popular or organized group pressure is evident from the fact that in the roughly 2,100 pages of hearings on the social security bill reported by the Senate Finance Committee and the House Ways and Means Committee, aid to dependent children is mentioned on only a handful of pages.

But to appreciate the full play of forces shaping ADC policy one must consider not only the public statements of the reformers but also the economic, political, and fiscal context in which the program was spawned. Politically, ADC had become lost in the debate over the all-inclusive retirement insurance program (now called social security), which conservatives, Republicans, private pension plans, and the private insurance industry were vigorously opposing. For Republicans the preferred alternative to social security was public assistance, which would not insure everyone but would help only the truly needy.[27] But if public assistance was better than social security, then Republicans could hardly attack the old-age assistance and ADC programs, quintessential examples of public assistance programs.

The fiscal aspect of the issue in these economically depressed times was equally compelling. Federal aid had strong support from state and local officials, whose fiscal problems had become increasingly desperate as the Depression had deepened. Indeed, one of the main justifications for ADC was that the Depression had left state and local governments too "financially embarrassed" to fund mothers' pensions by themselves.[28] The FERA had already been absorbing state responsibilities in this area, and ADC would systematize a practice that had already been established. In the words of the committee:

Due to the present financial difficulty in which many states find themselves, far more . . . children are on the relief lists than are in receipt of children's aid benefits. . . . We believe that the children's aid plan is the method which will best care for their

27. Derthick, *Policymaking for Social Security,* pp. 280–81.
28. *Economic Security Act,* Hearings (House), p. 159.

needs. We recommend federal grants-in-aid on the basis of one-half the State and local expenditures for this purpose (one-third the entire cost).

Such Federal grants-in-aid are a new departure, but ... the amount of money required is less than the amount now given to families of this character by the Federal Government by the less desirable route of emergency relief.[29]

The fiscal issue, the uncertainties created by the economic depression, and Republican and conservative endorsement of public assistance rather than social insurance were probably more decisive than the analyses of professional reformers in the easy passage of a federally supported ADC program. Congress was too much a product of a decentralized political system to alter federal-state relationships this quietly except in extraordinary circumstances. And despite little vocal opposition, there is evidence from the legislation itself that conservative members of Congress approached this innovation in federal-state relations with considerable trepidation. Instead of placing a minimum benefit requirement on states participating in the program, Congress did the opposite. Ignoring the CES's recommendation to leave complete discretion to the states, Congress limited the federal contribution to $6 a month for the first child and $4 a month for other children. When Secretary of Labor Frances Perkins opposed placing this limitation on state discretion, she was assured by the chairman of the Senate Finance Committee that it was all right to set benefit levels low initially, because future Congresses could easily increase them.[30] The cost was expected to be no more than $25 million annually.

The legislation had other defects. The aid went only to dependent children; no money was provided for the caretaker of these children. It was not until 1950 that the caretaker was counted among the recipients, increasing the official size of the family and therefore the amount of the grant the family could receive. And it was not until 1962 that a family with two parents could receive aid if both were unemployed. With these changes the program became known

29. *Congressional Record,* January 17, 1935, p. 548.
30. Witte, *Development of the Social Security Act,* p. 164.

by its contemporary appellation, aid to families with dependent children (AFDC).

Federal guidelines also allowed states to continue to impose the one-year residency requirement that had been a feature of the mothers' pension laws, and most of the states continued to impose the residency requirement for the next thirty years.[31] Residency requirements eventually became a contentious political issue, as reformers attempted to persuade both state policymakers and members of Congress that the requirement deprived many poor people from needed assistance. In 1969 the Supreme Court declared the residency requirement to be so arbitrary as to constitute a violation of the equal protection clause. In this way, the issue was removed from state and national politics and residency requirements disappeared from the AFDC program.

Since state control over residency requirements, benefit levels, and most other features of the program was scarcely questioned in the 1930s by any of those participating in the design of ADC, it could appear that the creation of ADC was more of a technical correction than a fundamental reordering of welfare priorities. Some analysts have even argued that ADC had a negative effect on the poor, because they received less under ADC than they had received from the FERA.[32] It is true that the FERA, by bankrolling state and local government public assistance programs, paved the way for the new federally assisted approach to social security recommended by the CES. But to treat the institutionalization of the new welfare state as a step backward from the FERA overlooks the fact that the emergency relief program was never designed or expected to become permanent, and programs that would replace it, such as ADC, would inevitably be more firmly embedded in the country's political and administrative framework. ADC is more accurately compared with the mothers' pensions that it replaced. The new law required that the states pay one-third of the costs and that federal "grants . . . be made conditional on passage and enforcement of mandatory State laws and on the submission of approved plans

---

31. Gilbert Y. Steiner, *Social Insecurity: The Politics of Welfare* (Rand McNally, 1966), p. 133.

32. Piven and Cloward, *Regulating the Poor,* chap. 3.

assuring minimum standards in investigation, amounts of grants and administration."[33] Thus the program reduced variation *within* states even though it did little to alter variation in benefit levels *among* them. And it compelled states to pay a substantial share of the total costs rather than shoving most of the burden on to the counties, a unit of government even more ill equipped than the states to finance a welfare program.[34]

Further Attempts to Standardize ADC

If the ADC program, for all its defects, constituted a major advance beyond the mothers' pension laws, the ink was hardly dry on the Social Security Act of 1935 before reformers began to pursue three separate strategies designed to establish more uniform state policies. First, reformers adjusted the benefits formula to give low-benefit states additional financial incentives to raise their benefits. Second, efforts were made to mandate a national minimum benefit. Third, a supplemental program, food stamps, was designed to offset variations in state policies.[35]

The politics of these reforms continued along much the same lines that had emerged during the New Deal period. When reformers were successful, it was because they were able to build a broad bipartisan coalition. When reformers failed, it was primarily due to conservative opposition from both Republicans and southern Democrats, who resisted an expansive, centralizing welfare state.

33. *Congressional Record,* January 17, 1935, p. 548.

34. As the CES stated: "Like the State fund in relation to the counties, a Federal fund would be an instrument for improving standards in backward States and would tend to equalize costs." CES, *Social Security in America,* p. 248.

35. A second supplemental program, medicaid, also reduced interstate variations in welfare benefits. Although medicaid benefits vary from state to state, they are subject to stricter federal regulation than are AFDC benefits. Since interpreting the value of medicaid benefits to recipients can only be done by making a number of problematic assumptions, and since the relationship between medicaid benefits and cash benefits is not nearly as direct as the connection between food stamps and cash benefits, we do not discuss the complex questions raised by medicaid policies. On the variation in state medicaid policies, see *Background Material and Data on Programs within the Jurisdiction of the Committee on Ways and Means,* Committee Print, House Committee on Ways and Means, 101 Cong. 1 sess. (GPO, 1989), pp. 1127–53.

More surprisingly, reform also encountered opposition from liberals who were more interested in protecting vested interests in particular states than implementing a more broadly conceived approach to welfare policy.

Welfare reform was also shaped by the institutional inheritance that had evolved since the days of mothers' pensions. As a result, reform proposals often had perverse consequences unanticipated by their proponents. Legislation designed to increase benefits in low-benefit states simply rewarded the stingy states instead of producing greater uniformity in welfare practice. Legislation that attempted to establish a national minimum benefit encountered opposition from conservatives and liberals alike, both of whom expressed attachment to existing state policies in their part of the country. And laws that gave recipients more nationally funded benefits whenever state benefits declined induced an overall decline in state benefits.

Thus none of the three strategies had the success that proponents had hoped for. Reformers were able to secure congressional support for the first strategy (giving financial incentives to low-benefit states), but it had very little effect on the variation in state policy. The second strategy (establishing a national minimum) failed to win the necessary congressional support. The third (using supplemental programs) proved most successful in reducing interstate variation, but it provided states with a set of perverse incentives that lowered their contributions to public assistance.

Increasing the Federal Contribution

One of the first anomalies noted by early reformers was that the federal government was paying only 33 percent of the cost of the new ADC program while it was paying 50 percent of the cost of aid to the blind and aged not covered by social security.[36] The differences in the size of the federal contribution may have been due to the somewhat different legislative histories of these two components of the social security act, or they may have been simply due to the

36. *Congressional Record,* June 6, 1939, p. 6719.

greater willingness of Congress to help support the "deserving poor."[37] Edwin Witte observed that when this anomaly was first noticed by CES staff "those of us who were really interested in this latter aid did not feel that it was wise to raise the point, lest we lose this aid altogether."[38] This suggests that the power of professional reformers had had its limits even at the height of the Depression. But whatever the causes of the discrepancy, the welfare reformers in the early years of the program came to regard it as a serious issue worth further legislative attention. They considered it as the reason that in 1939 eight states (Connecticut, Illinois, Iowa, Kentucky, Mississippi, Nevada, South Dakota, and Texas) were still not participating in the federal grant-in-aid program. They also felt it was the reason ADC benefit levels lagged behind assistance for the old and the blind.[39]

The 1939 effort to increase the federal contribution received bipartisan support. The Republican minority report of the House Ways and Means Committee "heartily endorse[d]" raising the federal contribution to 50 percent so long as the increased funds that would be made available to the states would be used in liberalizing present benefits and in extending aid to those denied assistance, "rather than to relieve the States of any part of their present expenditures for such assistance."[40]

Reform proposals in 1939 also included recommendations that the federal contribution should be at a higher rate for poorer states that had less capacity to finance their ADC program.[41] Although this recommendation was not included in the reforms of 1939, the change was adopted in 1944, when Congress revised its maximum limit on welfare benefits by adopting a complex formula that provided three matching rates: the federal government would pay

37. The first view is held by Steiner, *Social Insecurity,* pp. 19–26. The second is presented in Katz, *In the Shadow of the Poorhouse,* pp. 236–37.

38. Witte, *Development of the Social Security Act,* p. 165.

39. Average monthly benefits per recipient for the elderly were $19.50; for the blind, $23.25; and for ADC, only $13.50. *Congressional Record,* June 6, 1939, p. 6719.

40. *Congressional Record,* June 6, 1939, p. 6700.

41. The Senate Committee on Relief and Unemployment made this recommendation in its report (no. 2, pt. 1, submitted by Senator James F. Byrnes on January 4, 1939). *Congressional Record,* June 6, 1939, p. 6684.

75 percent of the first $12 in benefits, 50 percent of the benefits between $12 and $27 for the first child, and 50 percent of the first $20 for each additional child, but no funds if benefits were higher than these amounts. In theory this kind of matching formula should have reduced the variation in benefits among the states, because the federal government paid a decreasing percentage of the cost as the benefit level was raised.[42] But the introduction of this formula had no effect on the variation in state benefit levels: the coefficient of variation in the monthly payment was 0.33 in 1940 and 0.34 in 1950 (see table 1-1).

A bipartisan effort to assist the poorer states was also undertaken in the 1950s, even though President Dwight D. Eisenhower was generally opposed to a greater federal role. "I believe deeply," he declared, "that the State and local financial responsibility in these programs should be strengthened, not weakened." Eisenhower even proposed gradually reducing federal participation in the financing of ADC.[43] Eisenhower nonetheless accepted a congressional initiative to increase the federal contribution by paying 65 percent of the cost of ADC for those states whose per capita income was less than the national average.[44] But this effort to help the poor by helping the poorer states once again failed to have the desired effect. Although, as Eisenhower said, the policy change instituted "the desirable principle of varying Federal matching of costs in accord-

42. Robert A. Moffitt, "The Effects of Grants-in-Aid on State and Local Expenditures: The Case of AFDC," *Journal of Public Economics*, vol. 23 (April 1984), pp. 288–89.

43. Quoted in Wilbur J. Cohen and Fedele F. Fauri, "The Social Security Amendments of 1958: Another Significant Step Forward," *Public Welfare*, vol. 17 (January 1959), p. 5. Arthur S. Flemming, his secretary of health, education and welfare, "strongly opposed" congressional efforts to increase the amount of federal assistance, threatening to recommend a veto if any such legislation were submitted to the president. *Congressional Quarterly Almanac*, vol. 14 (1958), p. 158.

44. Several relatively minor adjustments in the program had been made during the Truman administration. In 1951 Congress approved payment to an adult caretaker as well as to the children. In 1952 the federal contribution was increased from 75 percent of the first $12 paid to each recipient to 80 percent of the first $15, and the maximum amount of support it would pay per recipient was increased to $30. *Congressional Quarterly Almanac*, vol. 8 (1952), p. 140. Also see Gilbert Y. Steiner, *The State of Welfare* (Brookings, 1971), pp. 78–79. The maximum benefit was increased once again to $32 per recipient in 1956.

ance with the relative fiscal capacity of each state,"[45] the differences in the benefit levels of the states remained as large as ever.

Mandating Minimum Benefit Levels

Efforts to address the disparities in state assistance programs more directly through a mandated national minimum benefit had more difficulty. Although the policy won the support of a Republican president, Richard Nixon, it proved impossible to hold together a broad bipartisan coalition on behalf of a moderate proposal. Attachment to existing institutions, conservative opposition to a centralized welfare state, and liberal concerns about the potentially negative effects on benefit levels in New York, California, and other northern states combined to forestall efforts at national reform.

Even reformers' interest in a national standard was barely noticeable before the Nixon family assistance proposals. A Senate report did recommend as early as 1939 that a federally funded welfare minimum be established.[46] But during the early years of the ADC program, Congress was more concerned about limiting the size of the federal contribution than mandating benefit minimums. The limit on the size of the federal contribution was gradually increased from the level initially established in 1935 of $6 per first child and $4 for each additional child to $32 per person in 1956, but it was not until 1965 that the federal government agreed to pay at least 50 percent of the welfare benefit no matter how much assistance a state decided to grant.[47]

Nor was there much agitation for a national welfare standard during the heyday of the war on poverty. States were raising benefit levels, the Supreme Court was abolishing residential requirements, restrictive administrative practices were being modified, and welfare rolls were growing dramatically. But neither John Kennedy nor

45. *Congressional Quarterly Almanac,* vol. 14 (1958), p. 159, and vol. 17 (1961), p. 281.

46. *Congressional Record,* June 6, 1939, p. 6684.

47. This was done indirectly at the time the medicaid program was established. States were allowed to determine the size of the federal grant they would receive either by the traditional formula or by the same formula used for medicaid, which had no upper bound. Gradually, states switched to the medicaid formula.

Lyndon Johnson proposed a national standard or even urged an increase in the federal financing of welfare benefits. President Johnson did appoint a Commission on Income Maintenance in 1968 to consider a variety of plans to establish a guaranteed income put forth by such academics as Robert Lampman, Robert Theobald, and Milton Friedman.[48] And in that same year Douglas Brown, a Princeton economist and planner of the social security act, explicitly stated that "the time has come for a truly national system of public assistance, nationally financed and administered, with national standards adjusted to local conditions and requirements."[49] But it was not until the election of a presumably more conservative Republican president, Richard Nixon, that a national welfare standard was proposed as part of a broader welfare reform known as the family assistance plan (FAP). It recommended a minimum $1,600 annual payment for a family of four.

Although this newly awakened interest in a national standard had undoubtedly been spawned by the civil rights movement and the civil violence of the 1960s, the Nixon proposal was actually made at a time when protest was subsiding in American cities. It was enough out of phase with the ups and downs of the civil rights movement that some analysts regarded FAP as a plot to restrict benefits.[50] Admittedly, the Nixon administration was planning to simultaneously implement a set of conservative administrative reforms designed to reduce "fraud and abuse" by making more stringent efforts to eliminate ineligible recipients from receiving welfare.[51] And the family assistance plan (FAP) itself did have a number of features that were expected to make it appeal to conservatives. It required that all those receiving benefits make themselves available for employment or job training unless they were

48. "Guaranteed Income," *Congressional Quarterly Almanac,* vol. 23 (1967), pp. 993–95.

49. Letter to editor, *New York Times,* December 2, 1968, p. 46.

50. Piven and Cloward, *Regulating the Poor,* p. 32. Subsequently, these authors retracted this argument, claiming instead that the welfare state had become too entrenched to be dismantled by conservative pressures. See Piven and Cloward, *New Class War,* pp. 13–26.

51. Evelyn Z. Brodkin, *The False Promise of Administrative Reform: Implementing Quality Control in Welfare* (Temple University Press, 1986).

mothers of preschool children. But enforcement of this requirement would have been difficult, making it more a symbolic concession to conservatives than an effective barrier to assistance for most potential recipients.[52]

FAP also attempted to reduce the disincentives to work that were part of the existing AFDC program, which cut welfare benefits by one dollar for every dollar a person earned. The FAP proposal would have instead phased out welfare benefits at the rate of fifty cents for every dollar above the first $720 earned. Although this aspect of the proposal was presented as a work incentive that would appeal to conservative voters, it actually represented increased federal assistance to welfare recipients who had some earned income. The program promised to provide more generously for the poor in other respects as well. FAP would have extended welfare benefits to all poor families whether or not members of the household were working. And FAP would have established a national minimum benefit that would be received by all eligible families if they had no earned income. Although this national minimum was less than the size of the AFDC grant in most states, it would have raised benefit levels in sixteen states and reduced it in none.[53] The program might be faulted for not having been more far-reaching, but it hardly constituted a step backward.

The FAP initiative was the product of policy professionals within a newly elected moderate Republican administration who sought to design more efficient and effective approaches to reducing poverty than those enacted during the Great Society era. Daniel P. Moynihan had been selected as the executive secretary of the president's Urban Affairs Council, and from this position Moynihan, long concerned about the state of the black family, convinced the president that FAP was a reasonable, moderate policy innovation that could ameliorate a serious and growing social problem. The idea was also warmly supported by the secretary of the Department of Health, Education and Welfare (HEW), Robert Finch, who had been responding favorably to the negative income tax and other work

52. Lawrence M. Mead, *Beyond Entitlement: The Social Obligations of Citizenship* (Free Press, 1986), chaps. 6–7.

53. Moynihan, *Politics of a Guaranteed Income*, pp. 162–63.

incentive proposals suggested by policy analysts within HEW. Although more conservative members of the Nixon administration— including Arthur Burns, formerly chairman of the Council of Economic Advisers and the president's counselor with special responsibility for program development—questioned the cost effectiveness of Moynihan's proposals, the president saw FAP as consistent with his program of redesigning, not overturning, the Great Society programs of his predecessors.

As the first self-conscious effort to establish a national minimum AFDC benefit level, FAP was initially well received by the news media, the major labor and business interest groups, such broad-based, middle-of-the road organizations as Common Cause, professional welfare analysts, and leading members of both political parties.[54] The program also had support from organizations representing states and counties, because FAP promised considerable relief for state and local budgets. Indeed, in later versions of FAP this fiscal relief was expanded in order to keep the legislation afloat as it entered increasingly troubled waters. FAP, like the original ADC legislation passed in 1935, won support as much for the fiscal benefits it provided states and localities as for the benefits it provided the poor.[55] With a fairly broad but not particularly intense base of political support, the proposal moved quite quickly through the initial stages of the legislative process. After the administration's case had been favorably received at hearings held by the House Ways and Means Committee, the committee reported to the floor a slightly revised version of FAP by a vote of twenty-one to three. The legislation passed the House in April 1970 by a bipartisan majority of better than 60 percent, just a little more than eight months after the president had recommended FAP to Congress.

This was the high watermark for FAP and, indeed, for any legislation proposing a national welfare standard. Even before the House bill was sent to the Senate for its consideration, opposition was beginning to surface. The Senate Finance Committee, which would consider the legislation in the Senate, was reputed to be more

54. Moynihan, *Politics of a Guaranteed Income.*
55. Leman, *Collapse of Welfare Reform,* pp. 83–84.

tight-fisted than the Senate as a whole, and neither its chair, Senator Russell B. Long of Louisiana, nor its ranking Republican member, the very conservative John J. Williams of Delaware, had much enthusiasm for welfare reform. Some of the difficulties with the legislation that had induced many conservative Republicans and southern Democrats to vote against the bill in the House now became the subject of withering committee criticism in the Senate. The senators were able to identify several extreme cases in which the combination of cash benefits and other public assistance would give recipients a higher income than would be received by those making some earned income. Although FAP would have greatly reduced the frequency of such disincentives to work, no version of it that the Nixon administration could devise eliminated all such disincentives, leaving the plan open to charges of inefficacy and internal inconsistency.

While conservative critics were questioning the work incentive proposals, liberals criticized the national minimum of $1,600 for a family of four as inadequate. The National Welfare Rights Organization, in particular, stepped up its campaign against the program, arguing that only a national minimum of $5,500 ($22,628 in 1990 dollars) would be acceptable. In its view, the existence of a national minimum might reduce benefits in states such as New York and Michigan, where benefits were substantially higher than the proposed minimum (even though the legislation expressly prohibited this). At its annual convention, the organization resolved:

While this legislation would offer increased benefits for a few people in the South, some low income working people, and the recipients of Old Age Assistance, Aid to the Disabled and Blind, we must conclude that it is, on the whole, an act of political repression.[56]

As the debate in the Senate continued, FAP became caught in the cross fire between these competing lines of criticism. By a ten-

56. Moynihan, *Politics of a Guaranteed Income,* p. 514.

to-six vote, with three liberal Democrats voting with the majority, the committee rejected the legislation. Attempts to bypass the committee and pass the president's proposals on the floor of the Senate were decisively defeated shortly thereafter.

The Nixon administration continued to propose FAP for another two years, but political support for the reform continued to recede. Both Moynihan and Finch left the administration, and the planners who replaced them attempted to strengthen Republican support by reducing the minimum benefit level and increasing work incentives. But every move to the right cost FAP support from the left. As the issue became increasingly divisive, the president's support for welfare reform waned noticeably. When George McGovern made a guaranteed annual income a controversial component of his campaign platform, Republican enthusiasm for anything resembling a national standard evaporated, and discussion of the idea disappeared from American politics for the next four years.

The topic reappeared in August 1977 when a newly elected president once again included a national welfare minimum within a comprehensive plan for welfare reform that was even more thoroughgoing than FAP. In his program for better jobs and income, Jimmy Carter proposed to fold together supplemental security income (SSI) benefits, AFDC, and food stamps into one program; replacing them would be a national program of support with a minimum of $4,200 for a family of four whose head could not be expected to work and a national supplemental program for poor families with an employable head that would begin at $2,300 and would fall at a 50 percent rate for every dollar earned after the first $3,800. If jobs could not be obtained in the private sector, public service jobs would be provided.

This time congressional support for a dramatic, far-reaching welfare reform was even less enthusiastic. The new chairman of the House Ways and Means Committee, Al Ullman of Oregon, had cast one of the three negative votes against FAP, and his view of the matter had not changed upon his elevation to the committee's chair. Even before Carter's proposal had been announced, he had warned administration officials that he was "deadset against any kind of negative income tax or guaranteed annual income" on the

grounds that it was "unworkable and a political disaster."[57] When
the Carter proposal failed even to reach the floor of the House of
Representatives, the administration scaled down its objectives but
still proposed a national standard for AFDC recipients at about 75
percent of the poverty line as part of its welfare reform package of
1979. After adjusting the minimum standard downward to 65 percent
of the poverty line, the House approved legislation that would have
brought benefits up to a new minimum standard in thirteen states,
all in the South and Southwest. But, like FAP, the bill died in the
Senate Finance Committee, as Russell Long continued to oppose
any plan that would establish a national standard.

Welfare policy became less generous after the Reagan administration assumed office. Instead of expanding benefits and creating
work incentives through a quasi-negative income tax along the
lines proposed by Nixon and Carter, Congress curtailed the amount
that a worker could earn and still receive welfare benefits. All
income earned after the first four months on welfare (except an
amount set aside for child care and transportation expenses) had to
be taken into account in determining the size of the welfare benefit;
in 1984 Congress allowed a disregard of an additional $30 of the
earnings, but only for the first year the recipient was on welfare.
Instead of a national minimum, Reagan's proposed welfare reform
called for a return of greater responsibility to state and local
governments.

Despite the Reagan administration's preference for state and
local experimentation, further moves toward a national welfare
policy were proposed as part of the Family Support Act of 1988.
The legislation required that states provide assistance to needy two-
parent families, withhold court-ordered child support payments
from the wages of absent parents, provide transitional medical and
child care services to families leaving the welfare rolls, and provide
training or work opportunities for a specific percentage of welfare
recipients. Establishing a minimum national benefit as part of the
legislation proved to be more difficult. In 1987 the House Ways and

57. Nick Kotz, "The Politics of Welfare Reform," *New Republic,* May 14, 1977,
p. 18.

Means Committee actually approved a national minimum, but representatives from southern states vigorously opposed including the national standard in the legislation. The Sunbelt Coalition, a congressional caucus consisting of representatives from states in the old confederacy, developed charts showing how much each southern state's welfare costs would increase if the proposed minimum were included. Concerned about the fiscal consequences for their home states, the representatives threatened to defeat the entire legislation unless the minimum was stripped from the bill. Since southern Democratic support was crucial in order to pass legislation that was at that point opposed by the Reagan administration, the federal minimum was deleted from the House bill. Even further compromises were necessary before the measure could win the necessary backing in the Senate Finance Committee and avoid a presidential veto; thus the legislation that finally passed had none of the increases in benefits and few of the work incentives that had been the hallmark of the Nixon and Carter proposals.

Supplementary Support for Low-Benefit States

At the same time that the Senate was rejecting both FAP and the Carter program, an alternative strategy for reducing the disparities in welfare benefits among the states was having much greater political success. With the backing of a broad bipartisan coalition of liberals, Republicans, and southern Democrats, major changes were made in food stamp legislation and administrative regulations that helped to standardize welfare benefits and increase them, at least temporarily. The reform succeeded in part because it was portrayed as a program to feed the hungry and reduce farm supports and in part because it placed no new direct burdens on state governments. Indeed, the long-term costs of welfare to the states declined in the years following the enactment of the food stamp program.

The political success of the food stamp program was in many ways remarkable, since food assistance to the poor had historically been a good deal less uniform than AFDC. Many communities had not been participating in either the optional food stamp or commodity distribution programs, and, among those participating, eligibility standards had varied widely. In addition, many welfare recipients had not been participating in the program because they had to buy the stamps out of their limited welfare funds. To remedy these deficiencies, the Nixon administration pushed through legislation in 1970 establishing a single national food stamp standard higher than any currently in use in the states. Benefit levels were adjusted annually to keep pace with increases in food prices. The secretary of agriculture was given the power to set national eligibility requirements, which were also adjusted regularly for inflation. Congress also lowered the purchase price of food stamps, making them more accessible to welfare recipients. And stiff penalties could be imposed on states that did not operate a food stamp or commodity distribution program in every county.[58]

In 1977, while Congress was fighting over Carter's welfare reforms, it eliminated all purchase requirements for food stamps, making them a simple supplement to cash assistance.[59] In so doing, Congress for the first time effectively reduced the interstate variation in welfare benefits. The way in which this was accomplished was extraordinarily simple. The federal government simply distributed food stamps in inverse proportion to family income. The less income a family received—whether from wages, AFDC, unemployment benefits, or SSI—the more it would receive in food stamps.

A program originally conceived as a way of reducing farm surpluses has been turned into a national welfare program. The politics of this are revealing. Just as had occurred in the original ADC and SSI programs, the food stamp program was enacted quietly with bipartisan support as a small part of a larger piece of legislation. In this instance, the food stamp program was embedded within a farm bill, most of which had little to do with welfare policy. Apart from the legislative strategy, there were many reasons for the broad political support for the food stamp program. As a means-tested

58. R. Kent Weaver, *Automatic Government: The Politics of Indexation* (Brookings, 1988), pp. 100–04.

59. This innovation was initially proposed the year before by Democratic Senator George McGovern and Republican Senator Robert Dole, but it was defeated in the Senate Agriculture Committee. Kenneth Finegold, "Agriculture and the Politics of U.S. Social Provision: Social Insurance and Food Stamps," in Weir, Orloff, and Skocpol, *Politics of Social Policy*, p. 228.

program, it appealed to conservatives. As a federally funded program not requiring additional state spending, it was favored by state officials. This was especially important in the South, because it did not impose any special burden on southern states that had relatively low cash benefits. The stamps were also presented as a food program, not a cash transfer, and therefore they fell within the jurisdiction of the Agriculture committees, not the House Ways and Means or the Senate Finance committees. Family expenditures were limited to food, so government assistance was helping families with necessities, not luxury items. And because the program was promoted as a way of reducing farm surpluses, it won the support of a bipartisan urban-rural coalition that few welfare programs could achieve.

The program's success in reducing the interstate variation in welfare benefits is indisputable. But it also seems to have reduced the size of the cash benefits that states provide recipients. By 1990 the value of cash and food stamp benefits combined was no greater than the value of cash benefits by themselves in 1970. As food stamp participation became a universal component of AFDC benefits, state cash benefits fell by one-third below their 1970 levels, leaving food stamps to make up the difference. As one econometrician has noted, between 1968 and 1984 "for every dollar granted in the form of food stamps or medical coverage, AFDC benefits were reduced by a dollar."[60] The food stamp program was, of course, not the only factor contributing to the decline in cash benefits over this period. The Supreme Court decision eliminating state residency requirements increased state concerns that they would become welfare magnets and thus led them to reduce benefits. But food stamps seem to have had their own depressing effect on welfare benefits.

The mechanisms by which this seems to happen in state politics are twofold. First, state-level opponents of increased welfare assistance have argued that the availability of federally funded food stamps reduces the need for cash assistance. For example, opponents of New York Governor Hugh Carey's effort to raise welfare benefits

60. Robert Moffitt, "Has State Redistribution Policy Grown More Conservative? AFDC, Food Stamps and Medicaid, 1960–1984," Discussion Paper 851-88 (University of Wisconsin, Institute for Research on Poverty, January 1988), p. 48.

in 1980 made the claim that even though cash benefits had declined in value in recent years, gains in food stamp and other benefits had more than compensated for this decline. Under the circumstances there was no need to adjust cash benefits for inflation.

Second, opponents of welfare increases have argued that increases in cash benefits would only trigger decreases in food stamp benefits. Advocates of the increases in cash benefits have had to admit that some reduction in food stamp benefits was inevitable, but have countered rather lamely that the reductions would be only tempo-rary, because cost of living adjustments in the food stamp payment would eventually bring it back up to its current nominal, if not real, level. The conservative argument was so compelling in New York that in 1980 liberals, instead of providing a standard increase in cash benefits, gave a "special grant" to each welfare recipient to meet "non-recurring, unanticipated needs." It was hoped that this special grant would not be deemed income by federal administrators and thus would prevent a cut in the food stamp benefit. A year later a New York assemblyman concocted a second scheme to assist welfare recipients without triggering a cutback in food stamps. He hoped that by defining the aid as a "home energy related payment" that would offset increased fuel costs, the aid would not be counted by federal administrators as income. Opponents correctly criticized the measure as "an attempt to obviate and get around the Federal Food Stamp Act."[61]

The same strategy emerged in Texas, when several religious organizations, social work groups, and the League of Women Voters lobbied successfully in 1978 for a special nonrecurring grant to AFDC children. The main advantage of this nonrecurring grant, once again, was that it would not be regarded by the Department of Agriculture as income, which meant that the food stamp grant would not have to be reduced.[62] The device was resorted to again in 1981 and still again in 1982. That these subterfuges were thought by welfare advocates to be politically necessary reveals the political

61. Robin Herman, "15% Welfare Grant Rise Wins Passage in Albany," *New York Times,* May 12, 1981, p. B1.

62. Anthony Champagne and Edward J. Harpham, eds., *Texas at the Crossroads: People, Politics, and Policy* (Texas A & M Press, 1987), p. 287.

appeal of the conservative argument that increases in state-funded cash benefits would only generate cuts in the federally funded food stamp program. Although the cut was only one dollar in food stamps for every three-dollar increase in cash benefits, this 33 percent "tax" on the benefits of the state-funded program was more than many legislators wanted to pay.

Some policy analysts have argued—at least privately—that food stamps have "solved" the problem of interstate variation caused by a lack of a national standard.[63] And it must be admitted that the program has cut by one-half the interstate variation in benefits. But the mechanism by which this reduction has occurred is peculiar—it rewards the states that cut cash benefits with an increase (of one-third the cut) in the amount of food stamps a recipient receives. And it penalizes the states that raise cash benefits by cutting the food stamp benefit (again, by one-third). Thus the program only aggravates the competition among the states, and in the end makes much less of an incremental contribution to the well-being of the needy than it is usually given credit for.

The Increasing Federal Role

AFDC shifted gradually from a small, state-based program to a large, federally funded program. When the intergovernmental program was enacted in 1935, benefits were set at a low level, eligibility was restricted, and federal fiscal participation was one-third of the total cost. In 1938 fewer than 1 million children received aid under the program, and the death of a father was the primary reason given for establishing a child's eligibility. Its total cost in 1940 was little more than $1 billion in constant 1985 dollars (see table 4-1).

The program was destined to expand in the ensuing decades, albeit without much premeditation on the part of policymakers. By 1950, 2,233,000 children were receiving aid, the total cost of the program had increased to nearly $2.5 billion, and the federal share of the cost had increased from 33 to 44 percent. By the early 1960s

63. This point was made to the authors in personal conversation by a prominent supporter of the new "welfare consensus" that has avoided the question of benefit levels.

TABLE 4-1. AFDC Recipients and Welfare Financing, Selected
Years, 1940–88
Amounts in millions of 1985 dollars

| | | AFDC benefits | | AFDC and food stamp benefits[a] | |
Year	Recipients (thousands)	Amount	Federal contribution (percent)	Amount	Federal contribution (percent)
1940	1,222	1,016	32.8	b	b
1950	2,233	2,463	43.7	b	b
1960	3,073	3,637	59.9	b	b
1970	7,429	11,320	53.6	b	b
1975	11,067	16,824	55.0	25,607	70.6
1980	10,597	15,612	53.9	26,954	73.3
1985	10,813	14,957	53.7	26,513	73.8
1988	10,920	15,139	54.7	26,053	73.7

Sources: Social Security Administration, *Social Security Bulletin*, vol. 50 (January 1987), pp. 76–77; *Background Material and Data on Programs within the Jurisdiction of the Committee on Ways and Means*, Committee Print, 101 Cong. 1 sess. (Government Printing Office, 1989), pp. 559, 1107, 1118, 1126; and authors' calculations.
a. Includes federal money spent on food stamp benefits for beneficiaries who do not receive AFDC.
b. Food stamps not generally available before 1975.

the ADC program had become quite different from a small program
to aid widows and orphans. Sixty-seven percent of those aided
needed assistance because a parent was absent due to divorce,
separation, or imprisonment or because the parents had never been
married. Death of a parent, once the primary reason for eligibility,
now accounted for only 8 percent of the recipients. The average
state's monthly payment had increased from $231 in 1940 to $314
in 1950 and $413 in 1960. Over 3 million children were receiving
assistance, and the program now cost over $3.5 billion.

The federal government also began to limit to some extent the
choices available to states. For example, states were required to
deny aid to families with assets of over $1,000 and benefit levels
were limited to no more than 185 percent of the state-defined need
standard. A Supreme Court decision abolished residency restrictions,
a variety of work requirements were imposed, the food stamp
program was inaugurated and expanded, and by the 1980s the
federal percentage of funding for the combined cash and food stamp
program was no less than 73 percent. The Family Support Act of
1988 required that benefits be paid to needy two-parent families

and that transition benefits be paid to families moving off the welfare rolls.

As the federal government has instituted an increasingly demanding set of requirements and assumed an increasing share of the financial burden, it has tried in two different ways to reduce the amount of interstate variation in welfare benefits. Neither of these attempts has really worked, however. On the one side, adjusting the benefit formula so that the federal government pays for a higher percentage of the cost is essentially an attempt to bribe states—especially the poorer ones—to raise their benefits by increasing the amount of federal funding they get for each welfare dollar they spend. Those who do more for their poor receive more in federal aid. While this may have raised the overall level of benefits, it has not decreased the variation in benefits among the states.[64] On the other side, food stamps reward the stingy states. They are explicitly designed to reduce variations in welfare benefits, but have done so at the price of reducing the average level of welfare benefits. Apparently the most effective way to both increase benefits and reduce interstate variation is for the federal government to provide 100 percent of the benefits up to some minimum level. Attempts to do this have thus far failed to win the necessary congressional support.

The configuration of political forces that has shaped the processes of policy innovation over the eighty years since mothers' pensions were initially enacted has been remarkably consistent. Although the balance of power among these forces has shifted frequently, similar patterns of conflict have reappeared on several occasions. Increases in aid to dependent children have seldom been the proud achievement of trade unions, civil rights groups, or representatives of welfare recipients. The innovations have instead been the result of efforts by middle-class professionals and reform advocates. They led the mothers' pension movement during the Progressive Era, designed the ADC program in the 1930s, introduced modest amend-

64. Moffitt, "Effects of Grants-in-Aid on State and Local Expenditures," pp. 279–305.

ments in subsequent decades, and led the battle for major reforms during the Nixon and Carter administrations.

These policy professionals have had limited political clout, however. More important to program innovation has been the Democratic party's commitment since the New Deal to the creation and expansion of the welfare state. Most northern Democrats saw further extension of public assistance as part of the party's broader ideological and policy commitments. Additional support came from less likely sources. Although states have often had less than generous welfare policies themselves, organizations representing state and local government officials backed a reform of the AFDC program in 1935, 1970, and 1977. Each time they supported welfare reform because it would reduce the fiscal burden on their own governmental jurisdictions.

The Republican party has also backed nationalization of welfare policy on several occasions, despite its preference for local control and its suspicion of the welfare state. Presidents Theodore Roosevelt, Dwight Eisenhower, and, most notably, Richard Nixon all supported policy liberalization, and their support was reinforced by substantial Republican backing in Congress. Nor has Republican support been limited to those years when the party has held the presidency. Republicans concurred in the establishment of the ADC program in the 1930s, they favored an increase in the federal contribution to 50 percent in 1939, they endorsed the food stamp plan in the early 1970s, and in 1977 a number of Republican leaders proposed a plan that included a national minimum. This bipartisan support has facilitated the introduction of many innovations in the welfare system with relatively little political controversy.

The sources of opposition to welfare reform have also remained remarkably consistent. The South has always been less generous in its funding of welfare programs, and many southern representatives in Congress have opposed a national standard. Stronger support for higher levels of welfare assistance has been precluded by the region's historically depressed economy, its dependence on low-wage labor, and its racial divisions. And the conservative wing of the Republican party has regularly opposed greater federal control of welfare policy. President Reagan wanted to return more responsibility back to states and localities, conservative Republicans led by Senator Williams of Delaware led the fight against FAP in 1969, and House Republicans united in opposition to a more comprehensive welfare reform in 1988.

The combined opposition of conservative Republicans and southern Democrats has been most effective in defeating welfare reform proposals within the Senate Finance Committee. Both groups have been well represented within the committee, and committee leaders have typically been members of one or another faction. The importance of the Senate Finance Committee in many of the deliberations over welfare reform also emphasizes the way in which the configuration of U.S. governmental institutions has shaped the policy choices the country has made. A tradition of state and local control, reinforced by a sharing of policymaking responsibility between the executive and legislative branches of the national government, has given opponents of a national standard the political capacity to prevent policy innovation even when a president has tried to build a broad consensus in favor of the reform.

Opponents of change have been so successful in preventing the creation of a national standard over the past eighty years that it would be easy to conclude that political conditions in the United States preclude the possibility of enacting such legislation in this century. Yet over this same period of time aid to dependent children has shifted from a program funded and controlled exclusively by state and county governments to one in which the federal government pays for three-quarters of the cost. If a national standard were enacted, it would simply bring to a logical conclusion a direction of policy change that has had a long, if somewhat erratic, history. The feasibility of reaching such a conclusion is the subject to which we shall next turn.

Chapter 5

Establishing a National Welfare Standard

I F THE HISTORICAL development of the system of income maintenance in the United States could be ignored, we would propose a uniform national welfare standard administered by a national administrative agency that distributed funds according to uniform eligibility requirements. Under such an arrangement, poor citizens could move freely throughout the United States without temporarily giving up basic income maintenance and without being burdened by the time-consuming, demeaning bureaucratic procedures that must be negotiated each time a person initiates a request for such assistance. The poor would be able to pursue jobs, family reunification, and a better life as easily and privately as other citizens. Such an arrangement works well for the distribution of social security benefits; a similar arrangement is slowly evolving for the blind, deaf and disabled; and such arrangements are characteristic of the welfare benefit systems of most European countries. It would not solve all social problems, but it would be a clear improvement on the present decentralized, inequitable, inefficient patchwork of intergovernmental arrangements.[1]

Yet a number of practical difficulties remain obstacles to the immediate establishment of a uniform nationally administered welfare standard. If benefits are raised nationally to the highest level prevailing in any state, the costs would be higher than practical

1. Other proposals to make comprehensive changes in welfare policy include Robert Haveman, *Starting Even: An Equal Opportunity Program to Combat the Nation's New Poverty* (Simon and Schuster, 1988); and Charles Murray, *Losing Ground: American Social Policy, 1950–1980* (Basic Books, 1984).

politicians are willing to incur. If they are not raised to the highest level, benefits to certain families would be reduced, creating personal hardship and political difficulties. The allocation of fiscal responsibility between federal and state governments would prove difficult. States would resist incurring additional costs, and the federal government would be disinclined to bear the entire burden itself. Creating a new national administrative agency or giving major new program responsibility to an existing federal agency would cause unnecessary conflict and confusion.[2] The future of state agencies currently providing welfare services would be cast into doubt, fomenting uneasiness and opposition from individuals and institutions whose support the new policy would require.

But valuable steps can be taken toward a national standard by building on the current system rather than trying to start completely anew. Realizing that the choices this country has made in the past inevitably shape the choices that are possible in the future, we shall propose a more limited set of changes in welfare policy that still greatly reduce the gross disparities of the present system. We shall then discuss the political feasibility of this proposal.

A Moderate Proposal

We propose that the United States establish a minimum federal welfare payment of $250 a month (in 1988 dollars) for a family of three. In addition, each family should receive the same amount of financial support that states currently give welfare recipients. For example, if the current welfare benefit in a state is $300 a month for a family of three, and if the state pays 50 percent of the total cost of a welfare assistance program, then under the proposed arrangement the state would provide $150 out of its funds and the federal government would increase its contribution from $150 to $250, providing a total of $400 a month for the family of three. In addition the family would receive $148 in food stamps.[3] The federal

2. Martha Derthick, *Agency under Stress: The Social Security Administration in American Government* (Brookings, 1990), chap. 2.
3. This is not the place to present a full-blown legislative initiative in all of its details. In order to be offered as a legislative initiative, this proposal would have to

FIGURE 5-1. Current and Proposed Monthly Welfare Benefits
in the States[a]

1988 dollars

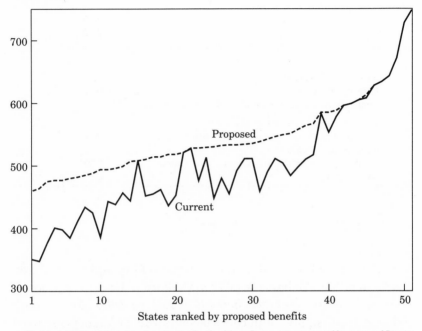

States ranked by proposed benefits

a. Combined AFDC and food stamp benefits for a family of three. Data points represent fifty states and District
of Columbia. See appendix tables A-1 and A-2.

share of benefits would be indexed to increase automatically as the
cost of living rises. For the first several years of the program these
adjustments should be greater than the cost of living in order to
offset past declines in benefits as well as any further declines in
the real value of the state-provided benefits.

Figure 5-1 demonstrates how this proposal would reduce the
variation in benefit levels among the states. It shows the level of
combined AFDC and food stamp benefits that a family of three
receives in each state under the current and proposed systems. In

be fleshed out in a variety of ways. Certain variations in state eligibility requirements
would have to be addressed, the amount received by families would vary by family
size, and other administrative and technical details would have to be worked out.

TABLE 5-1. Statewide Variation in Current and Proposed Welfare Benefits and Other Sources of Income

Source of income	Coefficient of variation
Proposed welfare policy	
Federal AFDC benefit	0.05
State AFDC benefit	0.50
Combined food stamp, federal, and state benefits	0.10
Current benefits[a]	
Federal AFDC benefit	0.30
State AFDC benefit	0.50
Combined food stamp, federal, and state benefits	0.18
Average manufacturing wages[b]	0.14
Unemployment compensation plus food stamps[c]	0.10
Social Security benefits	0.00[d]
Supplemental security income and food stamps[c]	0.08
Cost of living[b]	0.08

a. 1988.
b. 1985.
c. 1986.
d. Social security benefits are uniform across the states.

1988 these benefits varied (in the contiguous forty-eight states) from $348 a month in Alabama to $672 in California. Under the proposed plan, the lowest combined benefits would be $460 (for a family living in Mississippi); California's benefits would remain unchanged. Variation in benefits would be greatly reduced as the bottom end of the scale is brought up. A statistical measure of the amount of variation indicates that the proposed welfare program would vary to about the same degree as the current combined programs of supplemental security income (SSI) and food stamps (see table 5-1).

Under the proposed plan, no state would be paying a higher share of the total cost of welfare within the state than it currently pays (nor a higher dollar amount than for current AFDC payments). Indeed, most states would pay a significantly lower proportion of the total cost of the AFDC program (see figure 5-2). While the maximum contribution that any state pays would remain at 50 percent, the lowest share that any state would pay would fall to less than 9 percent.

This proposal has a number of political and policy virtues that make it more acceptable in the current political climate than a

FIGURE 5-2. Current and Proposed State Contributions
to AFDC Benefits[a]

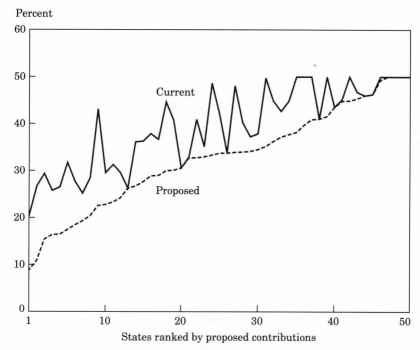

Percent

States ranked by proposed contributions

a. State matching rate in fifty states and District of Columbia.

uniform national standard might be. First, the proposed change
would increase combined federal and state AFDC benefits in the
average state moderately from $328 to $391 (table 5-2). Since food
stamp benefits fall with increases in cash benefits, the average
combined cash and food stamp benefit would increase to a lesser
degree (from $501 to $541). The proposal would also increase the
welfare benefits of nearly two-thirds of the families receiving welfare
assistance since 63 percent of the families receiving AFDC benefits
in 1988 were living in states where the federal share was less than
$250. It would not reduce the benefit levels of any family. The
estimated costs and benefits of these proposed changes in AFDC
are presented for each state in the tables in appendix E.[4]

4. It would be desirable to establish a minimum standard of need at the same
time a minimum benefits standard is established.

TABLE 5-2. Costs and Benefits of Current and Proposed Welfare Arrangements

Costs and benefits	1988	Proposed
Benefit levels (1988 dollars)[a]		
Federal	192	255
State	136	136
Food stamp	173	151
Combined federal, state, and food stamp	501	541
Combined benefits as percentage of poverty line	63	68
Families enrolled (thousands)[b]	3,690	3,833
Costs (billions of 1988 dollars)		
Federal	9.1	12.0
State	7.5	7.7
Food stamp	5.8	5.4
Combined federal, state, and food stamp	22.3	25.0
Administrative (AFDC)	2.4	2.4

Source: *Background Material and Data on Programs within the Jurisdiction of the Committee on Ways and Means*, Committee Print, House Committee on Ways and Means, 101 Cong. 1 sess. (Government Printing Office, 1989), pp. 540, 551–58, 1118; and authors' calculations.
a. Unweighted state average monthly benefits for a family of three.
b. Average monthly caseload.

The consequences of the reform for state-level decisions cannot be completely predicted. Although the proposal might seem to restrict state policy choices because it does not allow states to cut their benefit levels, very few states ever actually do so. Instead, most states have reduced real welfare benefit levels by letting inflation erode their value. They may continue to do this if they choose. But we think that states will be under less pressure to let real benefits shrink because a national minimum benefit will ease their fears that they will become welfare magnets. Critics who suggest that our proposal will encourage conservative groups to veto increases in state welfare benefits should remember that this is exactly what happened during the 1970s and 1980s in the absence of such a standard.

A second virtue is that the immediate additional cost to the federal government for AFDC and food stamps would be just $2.5 billion (table 5-2),[5] about a 10 percent increase in expenditures but

5. The additional cost for AFDC would be $2.9 billion, but there would be a $0.4 billion savings in the cost for food stamps.

a smaller amount than the Bush administration has proposed for its war on drugs. Even at a time when budget balancing and tax cuts remain central to political debates in Washington, the size of this initiative is not so large as to preclude public deliberation.

Third, it would reduce disparities in benefit levels among the states without raising the maximum benefit level in the ten states that currently provide the most generous benefits. Higher benefits may reduce work incentives, and any substantial increase might adversely affect labor participation rates among low-income people. But our proposal does not increase the highest benefits available through the welfare system, although there would be substantial increases for recipients in low-benefit states. Furthermore, those living in high-benefit states would have fewer incentives to stay there rather than move to places where job opportunities may be greater.

Fourth, states would still have a good deal of discretion over their own state welfare funds. The changes that we are proposing can be implemented without any changes in the benefits states pay from their own resources. Admittedly, states will be unable to reduce the benefit levels currently provided, but they will not be required to increase them. The federal government will bear 95 percent of the cost of the proposal; any increased costs to the states will be a function of increases in the number of poor people who become eligible for welfare assistance as benefits increase.[6]

Fifth, federal money would be spent for national purposes. It serves no clear national objective for the federal government to pay a three-person family enrolled in the AFDC program an average of $94 a month if they live in Mississippi and $311 if they live in Vermont. Yet this is what happens under current federal policy. The federal government treats its citizens differently depending on where they live simply because states have differing views of appropriate welfare benefits. Under our proposal, the national minimum would be set in such a way that federal dollars would supplement, not substitute, for state dollars.[7]

6. We are assuming here that federal requirements will mandate changes in eligibility standards proportionate to the changes in the new benefit levels.

7. In the long run, state benefits could fail to keep pace with the cost of living. We address this point below.

Past federal efforts to increase welfare benefits have tried to relieve the costs to the states by increasing the federal share of the total cost of assistance. In 1989 the federal share was as high as 80 percent of the total cost of welfare in states with the lowest per capita income. Such a policy provides a certain amount of territorial redistribution, helping out areas where average incomes are low. But this policy has done very little for poor people themselves; it has simply substituted federal dollars for state dollars without significantly affecting the benefits welfare recipients in low-income states receive. Our proposal redirects federal aid from places to people. Federal spending would be designed to aid families, not simply provide fiscal relief to the states.

Sixth, benefits will increase automatically with changes in the cost of living. State-determined benefit levels have fallen in recent years because state policymakers have failed to adjust them to keep pace with inflation. Our proposal would not require states to index their benefit levels. States would resist such a proposal as an unwarranted federal intrusion into their own decisionmaking processes. But without an indexing requirement, states will probably continue to let their benefit levels fall—just as they have let SSI and AFDC benefits fall in the past two decades. Therefore, the federal share of the welfare benefit should be adjusted at a rate at least 5 percent higher than the rate of inflation for the first several years. Such a policy would reverse the prolonged decline in benefit levels and offset further declines in the real value of state-provided benefits. It would also be a mechanism by which the country could gradually move closer to a national welfare standard (much as is currently occurring in the SSI program).

While we are proposing annual adjustments in the cost of living nationally, we do not see good reasons for complicating the program by providing for adjustments in benefits based on differences in the cost of living across states. The practical costs of doing so greatly outweigh any benefits that might be achieved. The cost of living varies more within states than it does between them. High-cost areas such as Boston, New York City, and San Francisco are located within the same states as much lower-cost towns, such as Fall River, Buffalo, and Visalia. Since welfare benefits usually do not take into account these intrastate differences in the cost of living,[8] it seems unnecessary to devise a complicated scheme that could make constant difficult interstate adjustments. Furthermore, social security, other retirement programs, and SSI do not currently adjust benefits for interstate cost differences; introducing this complication into welfare assistance would simply emphasize again the differential treatment this group receives. Finally, interstate cost of living adjustments would simply perpetuate the old system that encourages individuals to make their residential choices on the basis of benefit levels they receive. Any new policies should emphasize the national citizenship of all Americans rather than their particular residential status.

Seventh, our proposal can be integrated with other welfare assistance programs without great political and administrative difficulty. Currently, the medicaid and food stamp programs have somewhat less restrictive eligibility requirements than the cash assistance program, and a move toward uniform eligibility requirements for all three programs might be an appropriate part of the move toward a national welfare standard. Under current arrangements states must provide medicaid to families enrolled in AFDC, and most AFDC recipients are also eligible for food stamps.[9]

Many states also provide medicaid and food stamps to poor people not eligible for cash assistance. But in other states, raising the AFDC benefit levels may increase the number of families eligible for these programs, and some will enroll, thus becoming qualified for food stamps and medicaid. This will increase the costs of these programs somewhat.[10] However, because a family's food stamp

8. Intrastate differences in the cost of living were taken into account, at least to some extent, as late as 1989 in Connecticut, Louisiana, Michigan, New York, Kansas, Pennsylvania, Wisconsin, Illinois, and Virginia. *Background Material and Data on Programs within the Jurisdiction of the Committee on Ways and Means,* Committee Print, House Committee on Ways and Means, 101 Cong. 1 sess. (Government Printing Office, 1989), pp. 541–43.

9. In 1987 almost 83 percent of the families in the AFDC program also received food stamps. *Background Material,* Committee Print, p. 564.

10. Additional medicaid costs were estimated by multiplying the estimated increase in the number of recipient families times the average cost of medicaid expenses for AFDC families. We estimated that changes in eligibility requirements

benefits fall as other income rises, raising AFDC benefits will reduce
government spending per family on food stamps. In our estimate of
the overall cost of our proposal (table 5-2), we are assuming that
the relationship of these programs to the cash assistance program
is not changed. Under a $250 national welfare standard, food stamp
expenditures would be expected to fall by an estimated $381 million
a year. Medicaid expenditures, on the other hand, are predicted to
increase annually by about $300 million (not shown). The increase
in medicaid expenditures is modest because the national AFDC
standard we propose adds a relatively small number of new families
to the welfare rolls.

Finally, this policy innovation could be accomplished with relatively few administrative changes. We propose simply to increase
the federal participation in a system that would continue to be an
intergovernmental grant-in-aid program. Thus existing state welfare departments, receiving some funds from the federal government,
would continue to administer the program. While we have no
illusions about the inequities that may exist under the existing
state-run program, we also recognize that any move toward more
centralized administrative control would cause, at least temporarily,
its own distortions and dislocations. And evidence from other
programs suggests that new federal initiatives can be gradually
implemented through an intergovernmental system when professionals with expertise in a specific policy domain are in charge.[11]

Some people might favor using the tax system as an alternative
mechanism for achieving a national welfare standard. Tax credits
and tax deductions have traditionally been a more popular mechanism for promoting socially desired ends than direct governmental
expenditures.[12] The Internal Revenue Service (IRS) is able to collect
and redistribute large sums of money at little administrative cost
and in an indirect manner that is less demeaning to recipients of

---

accompanying the new federal standard would add 143,000 families to the welfare
rolls. The average family has one adult and two children, and the average annual
medicaid cost in 1987 for adults receiving AFDC was $1,047 and for children, $528.

11. Paul E. Peterson, Barry G. Rabe, and Kenneth K. Wong, *When Federalism
Works* (Brookings, 1986).

12. John F. Witte, *The Politics and Development of the Federal Income Tax*
(University of Wisconsin Press, 1985).

government largess. Because income is collected and distributed through the tax system, there would be no need for a separate welfare agency. There are no humiliating means tests; whether taxes are paid or credit is received is determined by the bottom line on the tax form. The administrator does not need to differentiate between the "deserving" (that is, working) and "undeserving" (nonworking) poor.[13] These features have made the earned income tax credit (EITC) one of the more popular ways of assisting low-income people.[14] Why not give the IRS and the EITC a greater role in the development of a national welfare standard?

Although an expanded EITC program might be a useful supplement to the proposal we are making, it is no substitute. It has many virtues, but it serves very few families now receiving AFDC assistance. The EITC provides assistance to working low-income people with children, not to the single-parent families that are primarily dependent on AFDC.

A family with little (or no) income receives little (or no) tax credit, and in 1988 only 8 percent of AFDC recipients reported earning any income.[15] Furthermore, if more than half a family's income is from AFDC (or another governmental support program), it is ineligible for the credit. While some of these barriers to an effective EITC program could and should be eliminated, there are other factors that make EITC an unlikely substitute for the AFDC program. Distributing relatively small tax refund checks (currently an average of $910 a year) is a far cry from delivering essential income every month. Making the Internal Revenue Service the welfare administrator of the country would dramatically alter its

13. For this distinction, see Michael B. Katz, *In the Shadow of the Poorhouse: A Social History of Welfare in America* (Basic Books, 1986).

14. Under the EITC the taxpayer receives a tax credit for each dollar earned up to a certain point; the credits are gradually phased out as income rises. In 1989, for example, a 14 percent credit was granted for the first $6,500 in income earned, so $910 was the maximum credit that could be received. After income reached $10,240, the credit was phased out at a rate of 10 percent, with all credit eliminated at $19,340. *Background Material,* Committee Print, p. 791.

15. A recent study has shown that many AFDC recipients do receive unreported income from other sources. See Christopher Jencks and Kathryn Edin, "The Real Welfare Problem," *American Prospect,* vol. 1 (Spring 1990), pp. 31–50.

goals and operations.[16] It is hard to believe that the IRS would welcome its new job as welfare administrator, and state officials and welfare agencies—not to mention the public at large—might understandably be reluctant to hand welfare programs over to the IRS.

The Feasibility of Welfare Reform

The case for a national welfare standard should by now be clear. But what about its feasibility? The 1990s do not appear to be an apt time for domestic policy innovation. Choice has been limited by the division of power in Washington between a Republican president and a Democratic Congress. Republicans have been opposed to tax increases and Democrats have been committed to defending social security and other politically popular programs; both are reluctant to support initiatives undertaken by the opposition. As was the case during a similarly divided government in the 1950s, domestic issues have become so partisan, ideological, and divisive that it has become difficult to build the large coalitions necessary to push proposals through the legislative maze. The fiscal deficit aggravates this partisan stalemate: any new proposal must be self-financing, funded by a fiscal scheme that keeps the expenditure off the official budget, or paid for by offsetting cuts in other programs. Any of these controversial choices provokes additional opposition. Policymakers are further constrained by a budget running on an automatic pilot set with taxes indexed at one of the lowest levels in recent times and entitlements indexed at a historical high.[17]

The creation of a national welfare standard appears even less likely than other domestic policy innovations. Proposals made by Presidents Nixon and Carter both failed to pass Congress. Early versions of the Family Support Act of 1988 contained a national minimum standard, but it had to be dropped to win a majority

16. Derthick, *Agency under Stress.*
17. Paul E. Peterson, "The Politics of Social Policy in the 1990s," in Joseph A. Pechman, ed., *Social Policy in the 1990s* (Cornell University Press, forthcoming); and R. Kent Weaver, *Automatic Government: The Politics of Indexation* (Brookings, 1988).

within the House of Representatives. The passage of a revised compromise version of this legislation, although only a modest revision of welfare policy, has temporarily provided lawmakers with the political cover that comes with the appearance of having addressed a problem. Lawmakers can be expected to be reluctant to take up welfare policy again in the near future. And the votes to be won by addressing the needs of the poor have seldom been crucial to the electoral fortunes of public officials.

But as pessimistic as these prognostications seem, it should also be kept in mind that policy innovation has often occurred precisely when prudent assessments of their likelihood have been most dismal. This has been true in areas as diverse as trade, education, and tax reform, and many astute and perceptive analysts have been mistaken about the possibilities for policy change.[18] This suggests that the possibilities for policy innovation can change rapidly with little notice by even well-informed observers.[19] It also indicates what is needed to break through the barriers that usually allow only incremental change. There are apparently at least five requirements for significant innovation.[20] First, some of the intensity of the

18. For example, a few years before the passage of the Family Support Act of 1988 William P. Albrecht said that "welfare reform will not be enacted by Congress; it is politically impossible. This statement applies equally to comprehensive or incremental reform." "Welfare Reform: An Idea Whose Time Has Come and Gone," in Paul M. Sommers, ed., *Welfare Reform in America: Perspectives and Prospects* (Boston: Kluwer-Nijhoff, 1982), pp. 15–16. In the same year that Congress enacted the tariff-reducing Reciprocal Trade Act of 1934, E. E. Schattschneider observed that "the American tariff is . . . firmly established in public favor." *Politics, Pressures and the Tariff* (Prentice-Hall, 1935), p. 283. Three years before the passage of the Elementary and Secondary Education Act of 1965, Frank J. Munger and Richard F. Fenno, Jr., observed that one could only reach "a pessimistic conclusion concerning the prospects for federal aid to education." *National Politics and Federal Aid to Education* (Syracuse University Press, 1962), p. 184. And a year before the passage of the Tax Reform Act of 1986, John F. Witte allowed that "there is nothing, absolutely nothing in the . . . politics of the income tax that indicates that any of these schemes [for eliminating tax loopholes] have the slightest hope of being enacted in the forms proposed." *Politics and Development of the Federal Income Tax*, p. 380.

19. For examples, see Paul Light, *Artful Work: The Politics of Social Security Reform* (Random House, 1985); Martha Derthick and Paul J. Quirk, *The Politics of Deregulation* (Brookings, 1985); and Theodore R. Marmor, *The Politics of Medicare*, rev. Am. ed. (Chicago: Aldine, 1973).

20. Compare John W. Kingdon, *Agendas, Alternatives, and Public Policies* (Little, Brown, 1984).

opposition to reform must subside. Second, economic or political changes must reveal growing problems that require policy adaptation. In the early 1960s, support for federal aid to education, which had seemed doomed by religious, racial, and ideological divisions, was instead enhanced by the growing presence of urban poverty. The result was the passage of the Elementary and Secondary Education Act of 1965. The inefficiencies and inequities of the federal revenue system, combined with an escalating fiscal deficit, brought taxes and tax loopholes to the political center stage. The Tax Reform Act of 1986, containing provisions long considered unachievable, was the result.

Third, a set of viable proposals must be regarded by the relevant policy community as an appropriate response to the problem at hand. Education was seen as a viable means of reducing urban poverty, and tax reform was seen as a way of lowering marginal tax rates and winning greater public confidence in the tax system. Fourth, the innovation should be seen as affordable. Aid to education was promulgated in a period of economic growth and fiscal surpluses; tax reform succeeded because it was revenue neutral. Finally, the innovation should command the support of the president or some other political leader who can command widespread public attention and political support. President Johnson emphasized education as a tool for reducing poverty, and President Reagan endorsed tax reform as a means of reducing the marginal rate of taxation. Both actions were essential to the passage of these policy innovations. For a national welfare standard to become reality, these five requirements for policy innovation must be met.

Waning Opposition

Although the pattern of conflict over a national welfare standard has been fairly stable over the past two decades, there is reason to believe that at least some of the intensity of the opposition has begun to dissipate. Support has come from the middle of the political spectrum—moderate Democrats and Republicans who favor an increase in welfare benefits above the levels provided in the lowest-benefit states. If the federal government is paying more than three-quarters of the cost of welfare, these supporters reason, then it should establish some threshold beneath which benefits should not fall. These moderates supported the Nixon administration's family assistance plan, Carter's revised welfare proposal, and a national minimum as part of the Family Support Act of 1988. Federal financing of a national standard was also recommended in 1985 by the Committee on Federalism and National Purpose of the National Conference on Social Welfare, cochaired by two former governors who became moderate members of the U.S. Senate: Republican Daniel Evans of Washington and Democrat Charles Robb of Virginia. Stuart E. Eizenstat, domestic policy adviser to President Carter, expressed the rationale for the committee's recommendations in terms reminiscent of President Nixon's defense of the family assistance plan:

> The federal government should have primary responsibility for those ... programs ... where nationwide uniformity, administration or finance are essential; where destructive competition between the states may otherwise occur; [and] where programmatic basic rights, such as minimum income support, are at issue.[21]

The support of these moderates for a greater national role is broad but generally not intense. Most supporters come from states where benefit levels are about as high as any national standard would initially be. Although their states may be in danger of becoming welfare havens, that issue burns in gubernatorial or state legislative races, not in contests for the U.S. House or Senate. Although a national standard could not be enacted without the broad support of moderates from both parties, their support is not sufficient. Until now, the more focused objections of opponents have dominated.

This opposition comes from three major sources. First, conservative Republicans typically oppose a shift in policy responsibility

---

21. Stuart E. Eizenstat, "Welfare Reform and a New Federalism," in *Work and Welfare: The Case for New Directions in National Policy* (Washington: Center for National Policy, 1987), pp. 60–61.

from the state level to the federal government, both out of a commitment to a minimal federal role and in the expectation that state-determined benefits will be lower than federally determined ones. Robert Carleson, former director of the California state department of social welfare and Ronald Reagan's appointee as U.S. commissioner of welfare, put the conservative case most succinctly:

> Welfare reform based on income redistribution principles and national standards would be harmful to the poor and disastrous to the nation. . . . Such a system would immediately become subject to political pressures, and the minimum benefits would be increased further and further, notwithstanding whether or not people were truly in need.[22]

These were the principles underlying the Reagan administration's recommendation to give the responsibility for financing welfare entirely to the states, and, when that proposal failed, to allow greater experimentation at state and local levels. Conservative Republicans can be expected to continue to support state control of welfare policy.

But moderately conservative Republicans may also come to see the advantages of a national standard, just as they came to support the program of AFDC for unemployed parents (AFDC-UP). Until 1961 families could not qualify for AFDC assistance if both able-bodied parents were at home; at that time federal legislation was modified so states, if they desired, could let two-parent families become eligible for AFDC. But by 1986 only nine states had created statewide AFDC-UP programs, though another seventeen had AFDC-UP benefits in some parts of the state. Only 6 percent of welfare recipients were in AFDC-UP families, in part because eligibility requirements were stringent.[23]

22. Robert B. Carleson, "State and Local Government Program Design and Administration—The Only True Welfare Reform," in James S. Denton, ed., *Welfare Reform: Consensus or Conflict?* (Lanham, Md.: University Press of America, 1988), pp. 43–45.

23. One parent had to have a substantial work history but could not currently be working more than ninety-nine hours a month. Julie Rovner, "Welfare for Two-Parent Families: An Old Issue," *Congressional Quarterly Weekly Report,* April 23, 1988, p. 1069.

The Reagan administration had long opposed making AFDC-UP mandatory for all states, threatening in both 1986 and 1987 to veto the entire budget if an AFDC-UP program was included.[24] Reagan and many other conservatives were opposed to making this a nationwide program because it was expected to add 65,000 additional recipients to the welfare rolls. Moreover, it limited state discretion when the president was advocating decentralization of program control.

Yet some moderate conservatives favored AFDC-UP on the grounds that without this program AFDC encouraged couples to live apart from one another. As Republican Senator John C. Danforth argued: "Why should the federal government give a penny to any state that is rewarding families for splitting up?"[25] This argument eventually persuaded even the Reagan administration, and the president signed into law the Family Support Act with an AFDC-UP program included.[26]

If there is some hope that similar considerations will lead some conservative Republicans to consider the merits of a national standard, there is even more hope that the opposition of southern Democrats will continue to wane. Historically, the South has favored less generous welfare policies both because of racial divisions and because many southerners believed the area's low-wage economy could be adversely affected by high welfare benefits. Southern states were among the last to pass child labor laws and mothers' pensions.[27] It was the senior senator from Louisiana, Russell Long, who helped kill both Nixon's family assistance plan and Carter's welfare reforms in the Senate Finance Committee, and many southerners in the House of Representatives opposed a national minimum as part of the Family Support Act of 1988. Of the fifteen states with the lowest

24. Mark Rom, "The Family Support Act of 1988: Federalism, Developmental Policy, and Welfare Reform," *Publius*, vol. 19 (Summer 1989), pp. 57–73. See also Rovner, "Welfare for Two-Parent Families."

25. Rovner, "Welfare for Two-Parent Families."

26. Although states must have an AFDC-UP program, they may withhold benefits from two-parent families for as long as six months a year.

27. John Clayton Drew, "Child Labor and Child Welfare: The Origins and Uneven Development of the American Welfare State," Ph.D. dissertation, Cornell University, 1987.

welfare benefits in 1990, thirteen were located in southern or border states.[28]

Both the economic and political situation of southern Democrats has changed in recent years, however. Between 1970 and 1980 the median income of both whites and blacks living in metropolitan areas of the South increased more than that of their counterparts in metropolitan areas elsewhere.[29] By 1980 the income in metropolitan areas of southern whites was within 4 percent of the white national average and the income of southern blacks was well above the national average for blacks. The need for special policies that take into account the economic peculiarities of the South has all but disappeared. Politically, blacks have become a significant force within the southern Democratic party while Republicans have mounted an energetic conservative challenge. As a result, southern Democratic leaders have tried to maintain a biracial coalition by moderating their political views, bringing them closer to the mainstream of the national party.[30]

Southern Democrats' view of a national welfare standard could be very much influenced by how a policy proposal is structured. If the legislation imposed substantial new costs on southern states, they would be very likely to oppose it. If the federal government paid for much, if not all, the costs of a national standard, then southern support is more likely. The politics of the policy initiative could also prove decisive. If it is proposed simply as a means of increasing welfare benefits for the poor, southern opposition could be expected. If it is sponsored by a moderate political leader as a rationalization of the welfare system and coupled with other features

28. *Overview of Entitlement Programs,* Commitee Print, House Committee on Ways and Means, 101 Cong. 2 sess. (GPO, 1990), p. 553.

29. Douglas S. Massey and Mitchell L. Eggers, "The Ecology of Inequality: Minorities and the Concentration of Poverty 1970–1980," University of Chicago, National Opinion Research Center, Population Research Center, January 1989, table 1.

30. This can be seen in the increasingly unified voting behavior of Democrats in Congress. See A. James Reichley, "The Rise of National Parties," in John E. Chubb and Paul E. Peterson, eds., *The New Direction in American Politics* (Brookings, 1985), pp. 175–200; and Kenneth A. Shepsle, "The Changing Textbook Congress," in John E. Chubb and Paul E. Peterson, eds., *Can the Government Govern?* (Brookings, 1989), pp. 238–66.

designed to promote work and family stability, then southern Democratic support could materialize.

The changing position of southern members of Congress on food stamp policy illustrates how opinion in that part of the country has moderated. Originally, most southern members opposed the program, both because it was an extension of welfare and because it did little to expand consumption of southern agricultural commodities, such as cotton and tobacco. Powerful southern senators and representatives were the main obstacle to the establishment of the food stamp program during the Johnson administration.[31] But by the 1970s most southerners were supporting the legislation, both because they discovered that the food stamp program helped to win broad support for agricultural commodities in general and because food stamp benefits went disproportionately to southern states— without costing the states any monies of their own.[32] In addition, the changing economic and political context of southern politics made it easier for southern Democrats to support this welfare legislation.

Opposition to a national welfare standard has also come from some northern liberals and poverty groups on the grounds that it would reduce benefits for the poor in large, liberal states, such as New York, which have had the highest benefit levels. The most intense of the left-wing opposition to the family assistance plan came from the National Welfare Rights Organization, which claimed

31. Key opponents included Representative W. R. Poage, the Texas Democrat who chaired the Agriculture Committee; Representative Jamie Whitten, the Democrat from Mississippi who chaired the agricultural subcommittee of the Appropriations Committee; and Allen Ellender, Senate Agriculture Committee chairman.

32. Kenneth Finegold, "Agriculture and the Politics of U.S. Social Provision: Social Insurance and Food Stamps," in Margaret Weir, Ann Shola Orloff, and Theda Skocpol, eds., *The Politics of Social Policy in the United States* (Princeton University Press, 1988), pp. 228–29; Jeffrey M. Berry, *Feeding Hungry People: Rulemaking in the Food Stamp Program* (Rutgers University Press, 1984), pp. 34–35; John G. Peters, "The 1977 Farm Bill: Coalitions in Congress," in Don F. Hadwiger and William P. Browne, eds., *The New Politics of Food* (D.C. Heath, 1978), pp. 24–25; Robert B. Albritton, "Subsidies: Welfare and Transportation," in Virginia Gray, Herbert Jacob, and Kenneth N. Vines, eds., *Politics in the American States: A Comparative Analysis,* 4th ed. (Little, Brown, 1983), pp. 382–83, 391–95; and Patricia Faulkinberry, "Federal Food Dollars Go South," *Economic Review* (Federal Reserve Bank of Atlanta), vol. 62 (November–December 1977), pp. 137–39.

that the plan would reduce benefits in New York, where most of its members resided. But in the twenty years between 1970 and 1990, New York welfare benefits declined by 37 percent,[33] a development that should give many poverty-oriented groups second thoughts about their opposition in 1970. Liberals backed Carter's welfare initiative, and they also supported a national minimum as part of the Family Support Act of 1988.

Growing Need

Not only is the opposition to a national standard moderating among both liberals and southern Democrats, but the need for a national standard continues to grow. Poverty is becoming increasingly concentrated among families with children, the very group that could be effectively served through AFDC. Poverty is also becoming increasingly concentrated within certain neighborhoods in large central cities. And yet states are under continuing pressure to lower their welfare benefits. A national welfare standard that gives poor people more residential choice can aid, however modestly, the increasingly concentrated child-centered poverty and at the same time ease competitive pressures on the states.

Poverty among children. Overall, poverty rates have remained fairly stable since the 1970s, but the composition of poverty has changed substantially. Among the elderly, poverty continued to decline in the 1970s and 1980s almost as fast as it had in previous decades. The extension of social security to virtually the entire working population, the increase in benefits, the indexation of benefits, and the provision of low-cost medical services have greatly reduced poverty among the elderly. The economic situation for children has been quite different, however. Poverty among children had been declining as steadily for the young as for the old in the 1950s and 1960s; in the 1960s alone the percentage of children who were poor declined from 27 to 14 percent. But the trends for the two groups began moving in opposite directions after this date. While poverty among the elderly was continuing to decline, the

33. This is the decline in the real dollar value of cash benefits in New York state. *Overview of Entitlement Programs,* Committee Print, p. 561.

percentage of children who were poor increased to 16 percent by 1980 and to nearly 20 percent in 1987.[34]

This growing poverty among children is caused in part by longer-term structural changes in the economy. In particular, the wages of younger, less-educated workers have not grown since the early 1970s.[35] Equally wrenching social changes have also occurred. The number of female-headed households increased dramatically between 1960 and 1985. Among blacks, the increase was from 21 to 44 percent, and among Puerto Ricans, from 16 to 44 percent.[36] These female-headed households are at much greater risk of living in poverty than two-parent households because the female-headed family is much less likely to have a second wage earner, because women (especially women with children) are less likely to be employed, and because women's wages are substantially less than men's.[37]

34. Mary Jo Bane and David T. Ellwood, "One Fifth of the Nation's Children: Why Are They Poor?" *Science,* September 8, 1989, pp. 1047–53.

35. Among males with less than a high school education the decline was by as much as one-third. Andrew Sum, Neal Fogg, and Robert Taggart, "Withered Dreams: The Decline in the Economic Fortunes of Young, Non-College Educated Male Adults and Their Families," paper prepared for William T. Grant Foundation Commission on Family, Work, and Citizenship, April 1988. Also see Clifford M. Johnson, Andrew M. Sum, and James D. Weill, *Vanishing Dreams: The Growing Economic Plight of America's Young Families* (Washington: Children's Defense Fund, 1988).

James P. Smith documents trends in poverty between 1940 and 1980, showing that the steady decline between 1940 and 1970 did not continue into the next decade. His explanation for the failure of poverty among black families to decline in the 1970s at the same rate as in prior decades is twofold: 30 percent of the explanation is due to the increase in the percentage of female-headed households; the remainder is due to the fact that "real incomes grew by less than 0.7% per year, compared to an annual rate of 3.9% over the previous two decades." James P. Smith, "Poverty and the Family," in Gary D. Sandefur and Marta Tienda, eds., *Divided Opportunities: Minorities, Poverty, and Social Policy* (New York: Plenum Press, 1988), p. 171. Smith does not consider the possible effect of falling levels of welfare assistance, but more adequate income maintenance programs for female-headed families could be expected to reduce the intensity, if not the extent, of poverty among this group.

36. Among non-Hispanic whites the increase was from 8 to 12 percent; among Mexican Americans, from 12 to 19 percent. Gary D. Sandefur and Marta Tienda, "Introduction: Social Policy and the Minority Experience," in Sandefur and Tienda, eds., *Divided Opportunities,* p. 10.

37. Marta Tienda and Leif Jensen, "Poverty and Minorities: A Quarter-Century Profile of Color and Socioeconomic Disadvantage," in Sandefur and Tienda, eds., *Divided Opportunities,* pp. 33–44.

Yet AFDC benefits declined by about one-third between 1970 and 1985. Some of the effect of that decline has been offset by increases in food stamp benefits and the availability of medicaid, but people dependent on AFDC assistance have not shared in the increase in national wealth that has occurred during that time. Unlike the recipients of social security and SSI benefits, AFDC recipients have seen all the federal increases in food stamp benefits fully offset by state policies that have gradually but steadily cut their cash benefits. Some may applaud this outcome, but it seems quite inconsistent with the broad direction of modern welfare policy. Indeed, it is even inconsistent with the welfare policies adopted by the federal government during the Reagan era.

The concentration of poverty in cities. Poverty was at one time a largely rural phenomenon. As late as 1960, household poverty rates were twice as high in rural areas as in urban ones (table 5-3). Since then poverty has declined in the countryside but has grown in the cities, so that by 1987 urban poverty rates were actually higher than those in rural locations. The pattern of this trend by decades is worth noting. During the 1960s the poverty rate was falling nationally, and in all types of communities the rate was declining. Although poverty was receding more slowly in cities, at least the direction was similar to that in other parts of the country. However, during the 1970s the rate of poverty in central cities grew from 10 to 14 percent, a 40 percent increase. Meanwhile, rural poverty continued to decline. The growth of urban poverty continued at a more moderate rate through the 1980s.

Not only has poverty become an increasingly urban phenomenon, but it is becoming increasingly concentrated among black Americans in a few neighborhoods in the largest cities. In the five largest cities, where this phenomenon is especially stark, the population living in areas with high poverty rates increased by 69 percent between 1970 and 1980, even though the total population of these cities declined by 9 percent.[38] Furthermore, the black poor within metropolitan areas are becoming increasingly isolated from other groups. The degree of isolation increased by as much as 12 and 11

38. William Julius Wilson, *The Truly Disadvantaged: The Inner City, the Underclass, and Public Policy* (University of Chicago Press, 1987), p. 46.

TABLE 5-3. Households below the Poverty Line, by Type
of Community, Selected Years, 1959–87
Percent

Year	Type of community		
	Central city	Suburb	Nonmetropolitan
1959	13.7	9.6	28.2
1969	9.8	5.3	14.8
1980	14.0	6.5	12.1
1987	15.4	6.5	13.8

Sources: Bureau of the Census, "Characteristics of the Low Income Population, 1971," *Current Population Reports*, series P-60, no. 86 (Department of Commerce, 1972), table 3, p. 35; "Poverty in the United States, 1987," no. 163 (1989), table 6, p. 24; and *Statistical Abstract of the United States: 1982–83*, 103d ed. (1982), p. 445.

percent in New York and Chicago, respectively, between 1970 and 1980.[39]

Poor blacks have become increasingly isolated in economic and social ghettos because de facto racial segregation has separated them from whites. Disconnecting welfare policy from residential location cannot be expected to change this deeply entrenched feature of American society. But it is unfortunate that welfare policy further limits the choices of the black poor in a society where those choices are already severely and increasingly constrained by the forces of class and racial segregation.

One need not romanticize rural poverty to recognize that intensifying, persistent, increasingly concentrated urban poverty poses a special threat to the social well-being of the country. Urban poverty spawns teenage pregnancy, withdrawal from the labor market, gang participation, drug abuse, crime, and violence. If a national standard could help those of the poor who wish to escape from the city, would that not be in the national interest as well as in the interest of the poor?[40]

39. Massey and Eggers, "The Ecology of Inequality," table 3. In a study of sixty metropolitan areas, these demographers discovered that the percentage of the black poor living apart from other social groups increased by 3 percent over the course of the decade. The trends are not uniform throughout the United States, however. In the West the isolation of the black poor has not increased, but in the Northeast and the Midwest it has increased by 8 and 6 percent, respectively.

40. These issues are discussed in detail in Christopher Jencks and Paul E. Peterson, eds., *The Urban Underclass* (Brookings, forthcoming).

The Policy Community Support

Contemporary social reform has been said to owe more to the efforts of policy professionals than to the power of politicians, vested interests, or voting blocs.[41] Welfare policy is a case in point. Aside from the short-lived impact of the National Welfare Rights Organization (NWRO), welfare recipients have seldom, if ever, been able to organize themselves into an effective lobby. If their interests are going to be taken into account, it will happen because middle-class professional organizations and policy experts give voice to their needs. These policy professionals, acting as surrogate representatives of welfare recipients, do not have the kind of influence to get legislation passed that is sometimes ascribed to them. Political leaders make a distinction between expert testimony and political clout backed by money, votes, and organized lobbying. But without the support of the policy community it is hard to see how a welfare reform program can be enacted.

Unfortunately, the welfare policy community has demonstrated little interest in a national welfare standard in recent years. The lack of interest seems to be due to three factors. First, the proposal was a central part of the ill-fated Nixon family assistance plan in the 1970s. At that time the national standard became caught in the crossfire between conservative opposition to higher welfare benefits and the NWRO's efforts to establish itself as a national political force by defeating the Nixon proposals. Policy analysts became wary of an issue that had no backing from the right and had become politically suspect on the left. More generally, it became ensnared in the dispute over the 1965 Moynihan report on the black family, which had become so racially divisive that most academics

41. Hugh Heclo, *A Government of Strangers: Executive Politics in Washington* (Brookings, 1977). This idea has been used to interpret the origins and development of the war on poverty. See Daniel P. Moynihan, *Maximum Feasible Misunderstanding: Community Action in the War on Poverty* (Free Press, 1969); and Lawrence M. Friedman, "The Social and Political Context of the War on Poverty: An Overview," in Robert H. Haveman, ed., *A Decade of Federal Antipoverty Programs: Achievements, Failures, and Lessons* (Academic Press, 1977), pp. 21–47. For another view, see Paul E. Peterson and J. David Greenstone, "Racial Change and Citizen Participation: The Mobilization of Low-Income Communities through Community Action," in Haveman, ed., *Decade of Federal Antipoverty Programs*, pp. 241–78.

and analysts found it safest to avoid the controversial topic.[42] And since Moynihan was the architect of the family assistance plan— which was supposed to address the problems of the black family that the Moynihan report had unveiled—the idea of the national standard somehow became tainted as well.

The debate over the black family has changed markedly in recent years. A taboo topic for more than a decade, it is now a major matter for research and discussion by sociologists, economists, and psychologists of all political persuasions. William Wilson's seminal study, *The Truly Disadvantaged,* not only revealed how political conflicts had questioned the legitimacy of scholarly research on the problems of the urban black poor, but also refocused the debate by showing how macroeconomic forces and government policy could shape family life and community cultures.

The debate over the family assistance plan had a second consequence. Numerous studies of the effects of welfare policy on residential choice of the poor were conducted on data collected in the 1950s and 1960s, and only a few provided evidence of a significant effect. One of the theoretical rationales for a national standard was thus called into question. The topic was virtually abandoned, and only a few studies of welfare benefits and residential choice have been conducted since then. But the legal context was dramatically changed by the 1969 Supreme Court decision declaring residency requirements unconstitutional. As welfare benefits became more available to newcomers to a state, the few studies that were being conducted began to reveal that state differences in welfare policy now influenced residential choice. As these findings percolate through the policy community, welfare policy professionals are again likely to pay attention to this matter.

Studies of the effect of welfare on migration fell out of favor for other reasons. Although migration studies may lead to the conclusion that a national standard is necessary, they can also be the basis for deciding at the state level against increases in welfare benefits. As we described in chapter 2, conservative state political leaders have used the welfare magnet argument as a reason for keeping state

42. Daniel P. Moynihan, *The Negro Family: The Case for National Action* (Department of Labor, Office of Policy Planning and Research, 1965).

welfare benefits from rising with the cost of living. Liberal, intellectually oriented politicians, such as New York Governor Mario Cuomo and Wisconsin Governor Anthony Earl, who commission studies and listen to expert advice before announcing their policy positions, have replied to these charges by claiming that the welfare magnet argument lacks empirical foundation.

In making this argument, these liberal political leaders are placed in an uncomfortable position regarding a national welfare standard. For them—or for the policy analysts to whom they have turned for advice—to call for nationalizing benefits leaves them exposed to a politically embarrassing inconsistency. On the one hand, they argue for a standard benefit because they fear becoming welfare magnets; on the other hand, when defending high state benefit levels they deny that a welfare magnet exists. Governor Earl could not resolve this inconsistency. He asserted that welfare migration was not a problem, then called for a study to see whether it was, and then said yes, indeed, it was a problem. The situation is not unlike the one faced by the child labor law advocates at the turn of the century, who tried to deny the reality that some fatherless families were dependent on the wages of their children. Eventually, they acknowledged this reality and then tried to address the problem by establishing mothers' pensions. Welfare policy advocates must once again recognize that their opponents' concerns are not a mere figment of the imagination. Once this is acknowledged, the welfare advocates can focus on what is needed to enact appropriate legislation.

Finally, the enthusiasm for a national standard has been limited by many analysts' suspicion that it would lower, not raise, welfare benefits. This concern was reinforced by the conservative tone in Washington during the Reagan era. As a candidate for public office, Reagan had long been critical of welfare programs, calling them wasteful and destructive of individual incentives to work. For example, during his first presidential campaign he criticized welfare abuses, telling an anecdote about a woman in Chicago whose "tax-free cash income [from the government] alone is over $150,000."[43]

43. " 'Welfare Queen' Becomes Issue in Reagan Campaign," *New York Times,* February 15, 1976, p. 51.

Thus he might have been expected to unleash a full-scale attack against these programs. At least as David Stockman saw it,

> The Reagan Revolution ... required a frontal assault on the American welfare state.... Forty years' worth of promises, subventions, entitlements, and safety nets issued by the federal government ... would have to be scrapped or drastically modified.[44]

True to his promises, Reagan proposed many cuts in welfare programs. He proposed to cap medicaid expenditures as well as to cut and deregulate education programs for the handicapped and children from low-income families.[45] He signed a number of such cuts into law. In 1981 he was able to secure from Congress changes in the requirements governing eligibility for AFDC assistance, a 1 percent cut in food stamps, a one-year delay in inflation adjustments for food stamps, and substantial reductions in low-income housing programs.

Nonetheless, most major programs aimed at the poor, the needy, and the handicapped were spared major reductions during the Reagan years.[46] Although the president was able to check the growth of these programs, he was not able to cut them back substantially. To counter Democratic charges that he was trying to balance the budget on the backs of the poor, Reagan promised to maintain the "safety net" for those who had fallen on hard times. Except for the marginal changes made in 1981, a Democratically controlled House and a combination of Democrats and moderate Republicans in the Senate fought vigorously to sustain safety-net programs, exempting many of them even from the automatic cuts required by the Gramm-Rudman-Hollings deficit reduction measure. Presidential vetoes were seldom threatened and never used on these programs. Democrats were unable to expand the safety net, but the

44. David A. Stockman, *The Triumph of Politics: How the Reagan Revolution Failed* (Harper and Row, 1986), p. 8.

45. Peterson, Rabe, and Wong, *When Federalism Works,* pp. 222–24.

46. John C. Weicher, "The Federal Budget and State-Local Responses," paper prepared for the Ninth Annual Research Conference of the Association for Public Policy Analysis and Management, October 30, 1987.

Reagan administration, despite its concern that federal programs were making the poor too dependent on government handouts, could not significantly reduce them or change their design. The outcome was to stabilize the programs as they had evolved by 1980.[47]

The viability of federally funded welfare programs during the Reagan years is by itself strong evidence that the poor will receive more generous treatment from federally determined programs. SSI benefits vary among the states by only a relatively small amount because the federal government fully funds a national minimum standard. This federally funded minimum has not only been indexed to inflation since the mid-1970s, but it was even slightly overindexed for a number of years in the 1970s, and in 1983 another supplemental increase was authorized.[48] As a result, the federal SSI minimum alone brought a single recipient's income to 71 percent of the poverty line in 1975 and to 76 percent in 1985. Couples receiving the minimum had an income close to 85 percent of the poverty line in 1975, 90 percent in 1985. Adding food stamps and medical insurance, a couple's income would have reached 106 percent of the poverty line in 1975, 100 percent in 1985.

It might be thought that the differences between SSI and AFDC are simply the differences in the way Americans respond to the needs of the "deserving" and the "undeserving" poor. Certainly, greater public willingness to assist the blind, deaf, and disabled than to help AFDC families could explain congressional readiness to set a national standard and assume federal responsibility for funding SSI while rejecting a national standard for AFDC. Nonetheless, the steady maintenance of SSI benefits since 1975 (compared with the decline in AFDC benefits) cannot be attributed just to the difference in attitudes toward these two different types of welfare dependents. More important is the fact that SSI benefits are federally funded. Indeed, state supplements to the federal SSI minimum declined by an even larger amount than did AFDC benefits. Although a few states (California, Colorado, Michigan, Minnesota, and Okla-

47. Paul E. Peterson and Mark Rom, "Lower Taxes, More Spending, and Budget Deficits," in Charles O. Jones, ed., *The Reagan Legacy: Promise and Performance* (Chatham House, 1988), pp. 225–28.

48. Weaver, *Automatic Government,* pp. 112–13.

homa) increased the real, inflation-adjusted value of SSI benefits for couples between 1975 and 1990, most states did not. In the median state, benefits fell by 50 percent, as states let inflation steadily erode the value of their contributions to the needs of the "deserving" poor.

Not only have increases in national SSI benefits greatly exceeded state increases, but coverage of those eligible for SSI benefits has been more complete since the program was placed within a more uniform national framework. In the two years after the national SSI program was put into place (1974–75), the numbers of blind and disabled recipients grew by 48 percent, a dramatic change that strongly implies the state-based system was not reaching many of those the program was supposed to serve. For the fifteen years after 1975 the numbers served continued to grow at a more moderate average rate of 3.3 percent a year.[49] All in all, the shift to a national program seems to have greatly aided the blind, disabled, and aged.

During the 1980s the welfare policy community has struggled to maintain federal programs created during the 1960s and 1970s. The effort of the major national interest groups has been so intense that they may be forgiven for not noticing that, at least with respect to the major entitlement programs for the poor, they were surprisingly successful. In fact, they were much more successful than their counterparts at the state level, even when the Democratic party controlled a majority of governorships and state legislatures. Hardly any more convincing evidence could be obtained for the proposition that welfare programs are more easily sustained at the national level than at the state and local levels. If the policy community can also put behind it the disputes over the Moynihan report and Nixon's family assistance plan and face the reality that welfare benefits and residential choices interact with one another, it is entirely possible that its interest in a national standard will be awakened once again.

49. The number of aged served also shot up by 27 percent in 1974–75, but from 1975 to 1989 the size of this component of the program declined by 38 percent, probably because social security coverage for the retired population has become increasingly comprehensive. *Overview of Entitlement Programs*, Committee Print, pp. 715, 728.

An Affordable Proposal

But even if the policy community regains an interest in a national standard, the goal of uniform welfare benefits cannot be achieved overnight. Political realities and fiscal pressures preclude dramatic alterations in a system that has changed only gradually over the past century. However, the costs of moving toward a reasonable national standard are considerably less than is conventionally believed.

First, it should be recognized that the current federal deficit can in no way be blamed on soaring welfare costs. In fact, the cost of cash assistance (in real dollar terms) has declined since 1975. The number of recipients has remained about the same, and the size of the payments per recipient has dropped precipitously.

Second, the initial cost to the federal government of the changes in AFDC and food stamps we propose is $2.5 billion, a substantial sum but within the means of the federal government even in the fiscally constrained circumstances of the 1990s.

Third, the possibility of financing domestic policy initiatives has been enhanced by the expected decline in defense costs over the next few years. Some have argued, to be sure, that the prospects of a peace dividend are greatly exaggerated. They point out that the projected defense budget over the next few years remains as high as or higher than the current budget. Such claims present the data in current dollars, ignoring the fact that in real dollars defense expenditures are almost certain to decline, especially after Congress makes further cuts in administration proposals. The peace dividend began as early as 1986 when defense expenditures' share of the gross national product began to fall. This decline in the most valid measure of the direction of government policy can be expected to be even steeper in the 1990s. There are, of course, many candidates for ways to spend the peace dividend—deficit reduction, tax cuts, education, infrastructure, health care, and space exploration. But the modest proposal set forth here is as strong a candidate as any of the alternatives; the fate of welfare reform depends not on fiscal constraints but on political realities.

Political Leadership

These political realities require that a national leader be committed to a national welfare standard. Although the first step toward reform is greater discussion within the relevant committees of Congress, a new initiative is not likely to be enacted until it becomes part of the presidential agenda. Even in times of fiscal constraint, the prospects for such an initiative are by no means hopeless. Five of the past six presidents have offered a major welfare proposal at some time during the course of their administrations, and four of the five called for greater federal responsibility and standardization of welfare policy. President George Bush should also seek a national welfare standard. He has done so before. As a representative from Texas serving on the House Ways and Means Committee, he bravely voted in favor of Nixon's family assistance plan in 1970. When he ran for the Senate the following year, he was attacked for this vote by none other than Lloyd Bentsen, who beat Bush by claiming that he was a liberal out of step with his constituents.

Now that President Bush has returned the favor, both can afford to take the statesman's position. The president is one of the moderate Republicans who could support a national welfare standard both because it would broaden the Republican party's appeal and because it is morally and economically sound. Senator Bentsen, as a senior figure on the Finance Committee, could be one of the southern Democrats who accepts a national welfare standard because it is good for his constituents and because it would help establish him as a moderate in touch with changing conditions in the South. If both agreed to work for this measure, the conditions for a broad, solid coalition would be met.

The changes we have proposed are not so much a restructuring of federal welfare policies as a recognition of the lessons of the past fifty years. In the beginning, aid to dependent children was expected to be a supplemental program that would be phased out as other provisions of the Social Security Act took effect. Its design, financing, and administration were left primarily to the states. Gradually, the permanent character of the welfare system became apparent to national policymakers, and just as gradually they have attempted to create a set of national policies. Federal regulation of state procedures has steadily expanded, and the federal share of the costs, including food stamps, has grown from 38 percent to 78 percent. The disparities that remain are anomalies inherited from an earlier era in which states were less affected by national markets, worker mobility, interstate competition, and Supreme Court requirements for equal access. A national standard for a national economy makes as much sense for welfare as it does for retirement insurance. As reformers explore ways to lift welfare recipients out of poverty, they need to consider the new case for a national welfare standard.

Appendix A

Early Research on Welfare Migration

The data collected before the 1969 Supreme Court decision took effect generally found small or inconsistent effects of welfare benefits on migration. In a review of the literature on welfare magnets, Larry Long observed in 1974 that "no study has presented empirical evidence for the hypothesis that welfare payments themselves have attracted large numbers of persons to states or cities with high benefit levels. Most factual analyses . . . have considered the hypothesis and refuted it, but the evidence presented has not been entirely convincing." Larry H. Long, "Poverty Status and Receipt of Welfare among Migrants and Nonmigrants in Large Cities," *American Sociological Review,* vol. 39 (February 1974), pp. 46–56, quote on p. 48. He draws similar negative conclusions from his own research. In a second literature review, Holmes concludes "differences in state AFDC policies have, at most, a minor influence on the residential location decisions of the poor." Martin R. Holmes, "The Economic and Political Causes of the Welfare Crisis," Ph.D. dissertation, Massachusetts Institute of Technology, 1975, p. 33.

Other early studies reaching inconsistent or negative results include Paul M. Sommers and Daniel B. Suits, "Analysis of Net Interstate Migration," *Southern Economic Journal,* vol. 40 (October 1973), pp. 193–201; Alan M. Schlottmann and Henry W. Herzog, Jr., "Employment Status and the Decision to Migrate," *Review of Economics and Statistics,* vol. 63 (November 1981), pp. 590–98; Gordon F. DeJong and William L. Donnelly, "Public Welfare and Migration," *Social Science Quarterly,* vol. 54 (September 1973), pp. 329–44; John B. Lansing and Eva Mueller, *The Geographic Mobility of Labor* (University of Michigan Survey Research Center, 1967); Gilbert Y. Steiner, *The State of Welfare* (Brookings, 1971); F. B.

Glantz, "The Determinants of the Intermetropolitan Migration of the Economically Disadvantaged," Federal Reserve Bank of Boston Research Report no. 52, January 1973; Robert D. Reischauer, "The Impact of the Welfare System on Black Migration and Marital Stability," Ph.D. dissertation, Columbia University, 1971, chap. 2; John F. Kain and Robert Schafer, "Income Maintenance, Migration and Regional Growth," *Public Policy,* vol. 20 (Spring 1972), pp. 199–225; and Gary S. Fields, "Place-to-Place Migration: Some New Evidence," *Review of Economics and Statistics* vol. 61 (February 1979), pp. 21–32.

A few studies using pre-1970 data did identify migration in response to welfare differentials. See, for example, Richard J. Cebula, Robert M. Kohn and L. E. Galloway, "Determinants of Net Migration to SMSA's, 1960–1970," *Mississippi Valley Journal of Business Economy,* vol. 11 (December 1973), pp. 500–05; Richard J. Cebula, Robert M. Kohn, and Richard K. Vedder, "Some Determinants of Interstate Migration of Blacks, 1965–1970," *Western Economic Journal,* vol. 11 (December 1973), pp. 500–05; and Lawrence Southwick, Jr., "Public Welfare Programs and Recipient Migration," *Growth and Change,* vol. 12 (October 1981) pp. 22–32. The Cebula, Kohn, and Vedder study has been criticized for its unit of analysis and lack of adequate controls. See Rishi Kumar, "More on Nonwhite Migration, Welfare Levels, and the Political Process," *Public Choice,* vol. 32 (Winter 1977), pp. 151–54; Richard J. Cebula, "Nonwhite Migration, Welfare and Politics—A Reply," *Public Choice,* vol. 32 (Winter 1977), p. 155. The Southwick study identifies as migrants all those born in a state other than the one in which they are currently living (thus requiring strong assumptions about the timing of the move and the stability of welfare differentials).

Appendix B

Definition and Sources of Variables

Definition of Variables

B = maximum welfare benefits for a family of four in 1985 dollars: AFDC (maximum monthly AFDC payments for a family of four) plus food stamps (maximum monthly food stamp benefits) minus 0.3 times (AFDC cash benefits less the standard deduction.) Data were for 1970, 1975, 1980, and 1985.

$\triangle B$ = change in maximum welfare benefits for a family of four: B_{j+1}/B_j.

$\triangle P$ = change in the percentage of the population in poverty: P_{j+1}/P_j. (P = percentage of the population below the official poverty line.) Data were for 1969, 1975, 1980, and 1985.

C = tax capacity index, based on "the amount of revenue each state would raise if it applied a national average set of tax rates for 26 commonly used tax bases. [This index] is the per capita tax capacity divided by the per capita average for all states, with the index for the average set at 100."[1] Data were for 1967, 1975, 1980, and 1984.

T = tax effort index, based on "the ratio of a state's actual tax collections to its tax capacity. The relative index of tax effort is created by dividing each state's tax effort by the average for all states. 100 is the index for the U.S. average."[2] Data were for 1967, 1975, 1980, and 1984.

PI = an index of political institutions in a state. PI = turnout (percentage of adult population voting for governor) times partisan balance (size of minority party in state legislature). PI can theoret-

---

1. Advisory Commission on Intergovernmental Relations, *Significant Features of Fiscal Federalism, 1985–86 Edition* (ACIR, 1986), p. 130.
2. ACIR, *Significant Features, 1985–86*, p. 131.

ically vary between 0 (where no one votes in a gubernatorial election or one party controls every seat in the state legislature) and 0.5 (where there is 100 percent turnout in the gubernatorial election and a 50–50 partisan split in the legislature). The actual data vary between 0.01 for Alabama in 1970 and 0.37 for Utah in the same year. Data were for various years; see data source.

$\triangle I$ = change in per capita income: I_{j+1}/I_j. (I = per capita income in 1985 dollars.) Data were for 1970, 1975, 1980, and 1985.

W = average hourly earnings of production workers on manufacturing payrolls in 1985 dollars. Data were for 1970, 1975, 1980, and 1985.

$\triangle E$ = change in the number of employees in nonagricultural establishments: E_{j+1}/E_j. (E = number of employees.) Data were for 1970, 1975, 1980, and 1985.

$\triangle N$ = change in the population: N_{j+1}/N_j. (N = state population.) Data were for 1970, 1975, and 1980, and 1985.

P_2 = a dummy variable for the second period (P_2 = 1 for 1975–80; 0 for otherwise).

P_3 = a dummy variable for the third period (P_3 = 1 for 1980-85; 0 for otherwise).

t = time period (t_1 = 1970–75; t_2 = 1975–80; t_3 = 1980–85).

j = year (j_1 = 1970; j_2 = 1975; j_3 = 1980; j_4 = 1985).

Level variables (B, T, C, PI, W) are data at the beginning of the period. Change variables ($\triangle B$, $\triangle P$, $\triangle I$, $\triangle E$, $\triangle N$) are ratios calculated from data in the first and last years of the period.

Sources for Variables

AFDC recipients: Bureau of the Census, *Statistical Abstract of the United States: 1975,* 96th ed. (Department of Commerce, 1975), table 490; *1977,* 98th ed. (1977), table 545; and *1987,* 107th ed. (1986), table 621.

AFDC benefits: Department of Health, Education, and Welfare, *Selected Statistical Data on Families Aided and Program Operation,* no. 4828-5, microfiche; Department of Health and Human Services, Social Security Administration, pub. 76-03200, ORS report, July 1975, p. 9, and pub. 13-11924, ORS report D-2, July 1980, p. 10;

and HHS, Family Support Administration, Office of Family Assistance, *Characteristics of State Plans for AFDC*, 1986, pp. 83–84.

Food stamps: Calculated from data and formula presented in *Background Material and Data on Programs within the Jurisdiction of the Committee on Ways and Means*, Committee Print, House Committee on Ways and Means, 99 Cong. 2 sess. (Government Printing Office, 1986), pp. 451, 456.

Employment: *Statistical Abstract: 1977*, table 656; *1987*, table 671.

Tax capacity: Advisory Commission on Intergovernmental Relations, *Significant Features of Fiscal Federalism, 1985–1986 Edition* (ACIR, 1986), p. 130.

Tax effort: ACIR, *Significant Features*, p. 131.

Wages: Department of Labor, Bureau of Labor Statistics, *Handbook of Labor Statistics* (December 1980), table 97; and *Handbook of Labor Statistics* (December 1985), pp. 218–19. When data were unavailable for particular states in certain years, values were estimated by examining trends in that state and in neighboring states with similar economies. Values were estimated for Michigan for 1970 and 1975; Colorado, Kansas, and Texas for 1975; Washington for 1980 and 1985; and New Jersey for 1985.

Population: *Statistical Abstract: 1987*, tables 24–25.

Poverty: *Statistical Abstract: 1985*, 105th ed. (1984), p. 457; Bureau of the Census, "Money Income and Poverty Status in 1975 of Families and Persons in the United States," *Current Population Reports*, series P-60, no. 110-13 (Department of Commerce, 1978); and Christine Ross and Sheldon Danziger, "Poverty Rates by States, 1978-85: Estimates from the Annual Current Population Surveys," University of Wisconsin, Institute for Research on Poverty, rev. February 1987.

Voter turnout: *Statistical Abstract: 1977*, table 809; *1987*, table 411. The following states have data taken from 1968, 1976, and 1980 gubernatorial elections: Delaware, Illinois, Indiana, Louisiana, Missouri, Montana, North Carolina, North Dakota, Utah, Washington, and West Virginia. Kentucky and Mississippi have data from elections in 1969, 1973, and 1981. All others have data from elections in 1970, 1974, and 1978. Values for the District of Columbia are for turnout in council elections.

Voting age population: *Statistical Abstract: 1975,* table 730; and *1987,* table 417. Data are from the year closest to the election. For 1970 the data for all states except Georgia and Kentucky are the population over age 21; for Georgia and Kentucky, population is for those aged 18 and over.

Composition of the legislature: Calculated from *Statistical Abstract: 1975,* table 724; *1977,* table 810; and *1987,* table 412. Values calculated for Minnesota in 1970 and the District of Columbia and Nebraska in 1970, 1975, and 1980.

Income: For per capita personal income, *Statistical Abstract: 1976,* 97th ed. (1976), table 644; *1987,* table 714; and authors' calculations from personal income data from Department of Commerce, *Survey of Current Business,* vol. 66 (October 1986), p. 47.

Constant 1985 dollars: Adjustments based on consumer price index, all items, in *Economic Report of the President, January 1987,* table B-55.

Black population: *Statistical Abstract: 1977,* table 35; and *1982–83,* 103d ed. (1982), table 36.

Appendix C

Alternative Analyses

The following results are not reported in the text.

Changes in Recipients as a Dependent Variable

We found that except for the time-period variables the independent variables (including welfare benefits) poorly predicted changes in the number of recipients on welfare. For example, when we substituted "change in the recipients as a percentage of the population" into the unlogged simultaneous equation used to predict "changes in poverty rates," we obtained the following (* = significant at 0.10 level; † at 0.05 level, and ‡ at 0.01 level):

Variable	Estimate	t-statistic
$B\Delta B$	0.07	0.7
ΔI	-0.74†	2.2
ΔE	-0.42	0.9
W	0.04	0.3
ΔN	-0.59	1.2
P_2	-0.22‡	5.1
P_3	-0.27‡	5.3
R^2	0.45	
SE	0.16	
F	15.9	

These results are fairly consistent with recent work by Moffitt, who argues that there has been a structural shift in welfare participation rates (picked up in our equation by the time-period variables) not accounted for by changes in the economy or the provision of welfare benefits. He suggests that this shift was caused

157

by changing attitudes toward welfare or a series of court and legislative decisions liberalizing welfare eligibility.[1]

Moreover, the number of current recipients in the population is not a good predictor of changes in welfare benefits. Substituting "recipients" $(R \triangle R)$ for "poverty" $(P \triangle P)$ in the equation for benefits yields the following results (from the simultaneous estimation using unlogged data):

Variable	Estimate	t-statistic
$R\Delta R$	-0.01	0.6
T	$0.23^{\ddagger}$	4.4
C	$0.13^{\ddagger}$	3.1
PI	$0.02^{\dagger}$	2.4
B	$-0.35^{\ddagger}$	7.9
P_2	$-0.12^{\ddagger}$	8.5
P_3	$-0.11^{\ddagger}$	6.5
R^2	0.52	
SE	0.07	
F	20	

Entering Welfare Benefit Levels and Changes in Benefits Separately

The estimated coefficients and summary statistics for the unlogged simultaneous equation predicting poverty with welfare benefit levels and changes in benefits entered separately are as follows:

Variable	Estimate	t-statistic
B	0.02	1.3
ΔB	0.16	0.3
ΔI	-0.53^{*}	1.7
ΔE	-0.64^{*}	1.7
W	$0.34^{\ddagger}$	2.6
N	0.43	0.9
P_2	$0.36^{\ddagger}$	4.9
P_3	$0.23^{\ddagger}$	3.6
R^2	0.55	
SE	0.16	
F	20	

1. Robert Moffitt, "Historical Growth in Participation in Aid to Families with Dependent Children: Was There a Structural Shift?" *Journal of Post Keynesian Economics,* vol. 9 (Spring 1987), pp. 347–63.

Entering Poverty Levels and Changes in Poverty Separately

The estimated coefficients and summary statistics for the un-logged simultaneous equation predicting benefits with poverty levels and changes in poverty entered separately are shown below.

Variable	Estimate	t-statistic
P	$-0.41^\dagger$	2.0
ΔP	-0.11	1.6
T	$0.17^\ddagger$	4.3
C	0.07^*	1.8
PI	$0.18^\dagger$	2.4
B	$-0.49^\ddagger$	7.5
P_2	$-0.09^\ddagger$	3.1
P_3	$-0.08^\ddagger$	3.2
R^2	0.52	
SE	0.064	
F	18.3	

Federal Matching Rates as an Explanatory Variable

The estimated coefficients and summary statistics for the un-logged simultaneous equation predicting benefits with the share of the AFDC costs (the "matching rate") that the states must pay entered as an explanatory variable (M) is shown below. Although other estimations showed the matching rate does have an effect on benefit *levels* within the states,[2] it does not have an effect on *changes*

---

2. Edward M. Gramlich and Deborah S. Laren, "Migration and Income Redistribution Responsibilities," *Journal of Human Resources,* vol. 19 (Fall 1984), pp. 489–511; Robert A. Moffitt, "The Effects of Grants-in-Aid on State and Local Expenditures: The Case of AFDC," *Journal of Public Economics,* vol. 23 (April 1984), pp. 279–305; Larry L. Orr, "Income Transfers as a Public Good: An Application to AFDC," *American Economic Review,* vol. 66 (June 1976), pp. 359–71; and Robert D. Plotnick and Richard F. Winters, "A Politico-Economic Theory of Income Redistribution," *American Political Science Review,* vol. 79 (June 1985), pp. 458–73.

in benefits, probably because there were few changes in the matching rates between 1970 and 1985.

Variable	Estimate	t-statistic
$P\Delta P$	0.39[†]	2.0
M	0.0002	0.2
T	0.17	1.5
C	0.06[‡]	4.0
PI	0.18[†]	2.3
B	-0.50[‡]	7.8
P_2	-0.11[‡]	7.4
P_3	-0.09[‡]	5.8
R^2	0.52	
SE	0.064	
F	18.1	

Use of Blacks as a Proxy for At-Risk Population

In estimations for benefits that included both poverty and black population, the coefficient for the black population was not significant. Below are the results estimated by substituting an interactive term for the black population (BP = percentage of population that is black, and $\Delta BP = BP_{j+1}/BP_j$) in place of the interactive poverty term in the unlogged simultaneous equation predicting change in the location of the black population. Because high-quality estimates of the black population by state are unavailable for 1985, the estimations below use data from 1970, 1975, and 1980. Hence the number of cases is reduced to 93. There is no period three in this equation, hence no dummy variable P_3. Fewer cases leave most coefficients below the level of statistical significance; the size of the benefit coefficients is nonetheless similar to that reported in column 3 of table 3-1.

Variable	Estimate	t-statistic
$B\Delta B$	0.26	1.5
ΔI	-0.30	0.9
ΔE	-0.19	0.5
W	0.14	0.9
ΔN	1.26	2.5
P_2	0.05	1.3
R^2	0.25	
SE	0.148	
F	4.9	

Below are the results estimated by substituting the same interactive term for the black population in place of the interactive poverty term in the unlogged simultaneous equation predicting change in welfare benefits.

Variable	Estimate	t-statistic
$BP\Delta BP$	−0.15*	1.7
T	0.22‡	3.7
C	0.11‡	3.7
PI	0.13	1.2
B	−0.47‡	6.4
P_2	−0.11‡	7.5
R^2	0.55	
SE	0.070	
F	17.6	

Using AFDC Benefits without Food Stamps as a Measure of Welfare Policy

An alternative measure of state welfare policy is the maximum level of cash assistance for which a family of four is eligible. Compared with the combined food stamp–cash benefit measure used in tables 3-3 and 3-4, this measure has the advantage of being a better indicator of the preferences of state policymakers. This level is determined solely by state officials, and it is the most visible indicator of state welfare policy to state politicians. We chose not to use this indicator in tables 3-3 and 3-4, because we expected that those at risk of welfare dependency themselves would be more sensitive to the combined package of benefits provided by food stamps and cash assistance together.

In the equation reported below one can see that the first expectation is correct. State policymakers make larger adjustments in cash assistance benefits in response to changing poverty rates than they make in the combined package of food stamps and cash assistance.

The estimation is the same as for column 3 in table 3-2, except for the substitution of A for B and ΔA for ΔB, where A = maximum AFDC benefit, family of four, 1985 dollars; and $\Delta A = A_{j+1}/A_j$.

Variable	Estimate	t-statistic
$P\Delta P$	−0.76*	1.9
T	0.31‡	3.6
C	0.10	1.3
PI	0.30*	1.8
A	−0.59‡	6.3
P_2	−0.08‡	2.9
P_3	−0.09‡	3.0
R^2	0.28	
SE	0.136	
F	7.3	

A comparison of the following equation with column 3 in table 3-1 shows the second expectation is also correct. Changes in poverty rates are slightly less sensitive to differences in cash benefits than to differences in the combination of food stamps and cash benefits.

Variable	Estimate	t-statistic
$A\Delta A$	0.20*	1.8
ΔI	−0.54*	1.8
ΔE	−0.63*	1.7
W	0.34‡	2.8
ΔN	0.43	0.9
P_2	0.35‡	8.8
P_3	0.22‡	4.8
R^2	0.55	
SE	0.159	
F	23.1	

Effects of Income

The effects of income on benefit levels are presented below from an estimate using an unlogged simultaneous equation.

Variable	Estimate	t-statistic
$P\Delta P$	−0.50‡	2.6
T	0.20‡	4.6
C	0.12†	2.4
PI	0.14*	1.8
B	−0.05‡	7.6
I	−0.01*	1.7
P_2	−0.10‡	6.56
P_3	−0.07‡	5.3
R^2	0.53	
SE	0.061	
F	18.9	

Appendix D

Variables Not Included in the Analysis

The Welfare Tax Rate

The rate at which welfare benefits are "taxed," that is, the proportion of the benefit that recipients lose for every dollar that they earn, has been used as an indicator of welfare policy decisions. The federal tax rate is the same for every state, because Congress has legislated the amount one can earn before welfare benefits are deducted. But states determine the size of the transportation and child care costs that can also be deducted from earnings before reductions in welfare benefits are required. States and localities may also differ in the way in which these regulations are administered.[1] Moffitt estimated "actual tax rates" by using reports of earnings and welfare benefits received in a 1975 nationwide survey of AFDC recipients.[2] Gramlich and Laren use Moffitt's data in their analysis.[3] We did not use this information because it restricts the time period on which the analysis can be performed, it is available for only thirty-five states, the data provide only an imperfect measure of true tax rates (as Moffitt readily concedes), and in Moffitt's own analysis, changes in the tax rate have "virtually no effect on the participation rate."[4] Southwick also finds that tax rates have no effect on migration.[5]

1. Irene Lurie, "Estimates of Tax Rates in the AFDC Program," *National Tax Journal,* vol. 27 (March 1974), pp. 93–111.

2. Robert Moffitt, "An Economic Model of Welfare Stigma," *American Economic Review,* vol. 73 (December 1983), p. 1025.

3. Edward M. Gramlich and Deborah S. Laren, "Migration and Income Redistribution Responsibilities," *Journal of Human Resources,* vol. 19 (Fall 1984), pp. 489–511.

4. Moffitt, "An Economic Model of Welfare Stigma," p. 1032.

5. Lawrence Southwick, Jr., "Public Welfare Programs and Recipient Migration," *Growth and Change,* vol. 12 (October 1981), p. 22.

Cost of Living

We did not adjust benefit levels for differences in cost of living among the states. When Gramlich made such an adjustment his results did not change from those using unadjusted data.[6] In his revised study with Laren, Gramlich explains, "Experimentation with this [cost-of-living] index in the earlier paper proved notably unsuccessful. Here we just ignored the issue."[7]

6. Edward M. Gramlich, "An Econometric Examination of the New Federalism," *Brookings Papers on Economic Activity, 1982:2,* p. 344.

7. Gramlich and Laren, "Migration and Income Redistribution," p. 505.

Appendix E

Welfare Statistics, Current and Proposed, by State

TABLE A-1. Current Welfare Benefit Levels, by State
Benefits in 1988 dollars

State	Average federal AFDC benefit[a]	Average state AFDC benefit[a]	Average combined AFDC benefit[a]	Maximum food stamp benefit[b]	Total benefits	Percentage of poverty line[c]
Mississippi	95	24	119	232	351	45
Alabama	84	30	114	234	348	44
Tennessee	109	46	155	221	376	48
Arkansas	141	49	190	211	401	51
South Carolina	137	49	186	212	398	51
Louisiana	114	53	167	218	385	49
Kentucky	147	57	204	207	411	52
West Virginia	178	60	238	196	434	55
New Mexico	161	64	225	200	425	54
Texas	96	73	169	217	386	49
Idaho	176	74	250	193	443	56
North Carolina	167	76	243	195	438	56
South Dakota	190	80	270	187	457	58
Georgia	161	91	252	192	444	57
Utah	253	90	343	165	508	65
Indiana	168	95	263	189	452	57
Arizona	166	102	268	187	455	58
Oklahoma	176	102	278	184	462	59
Florida	133	107	240	196	436	55
Missouri	156	108	264	189	453	58
Montana	251	111	362	159	521	66
Maine	248	122	370	157	527	67
Ohio	176	122	298	178	476	61
North Dakota	227	123	350	163	513	65
Virginia	132	125	257	191	448	57
Wyoming	176	127	303	177	480	61
Delaware	139	128	267	188	455	58
Nebraska	191	129	320	172	492	63
Iowa	218	130	348	163	511	65
Oregon	216	132	348	163	511	65
Nevada	137	136	273	186	459	58
Colorado	175	142	317	173	490	62
Pennsylvania	199	148	347	164	511	65
Kansas	187	151	338	166	504	64
Illinois	155	155	309	175	484	62
Maryland	165	165	329	169	498	63
DC	173	173	346	164	510	65
New Jersey	178	178	356	161	517	66
Rhode Island	247	203	450	133	583	74
New Hampshire	204	204	407	146	553	70

TABLE A-1 (*continued*)

State	Average federal AFDC benefit[a]	Average state AFDC benefit[a]	Average combined AFDC benefit[a]	Maximum food stamp benefit[b]	Total benefits	Percentage of poverty line[c]
Washington	236	207	443	135	578	74
Vermont	311	158	469	127	596	76
Wisconsin	279	194	473	126	599	76
Michigan	272	209	481	124	605	77
Connecticut	243	243	486	122	608	77
Minnesota	278	237	515	113	628	80
New York	262	262	523	111	634	70
Massachusetts	268	268	536	107	643	82
California	289	289	578	94	672	86
Hawaii	258	223	481	247	728	80
Alaska	297	297	594	154	748	76
Average	192	136	328	173	501	63
Coefficient of variation	0.30	0.50	0.36	0.20	0.18	0.16

Source: *Background Material and Data on Programs within the Jurisdiction of the Committee on Ways and Means*, Committee Print, House Committee on Ways and Means, 101 Cong. 1 sess. (Government Printing Office, 1989), pp. 551–53, 557, 1115.

a. Total assistance payments divided by average caseload.

b. Food stamp benefits are based on average AFDC payments and assume the standard deduction ($106 per month). Food stamps have higher maximum benefits and standard deductions in Alaska and Hawaii.

c. The monthly poverty threshold was $786 in 1988 for a family of three. The threshold was 25 percent higher in Alaska and 15 percent higher in Hawaii. In 1987 the average AFDC family size was 3.0.

TABLE A-2. Proposed Welfare Benefit Levels, by State
Benefits in 1988 dollars

State	Average federal AFDC benefit[a]	Average state AFDC benefit[a]	Average combined AFDC benefit[a]	Maximum food stamp benefit[b]	Proposed total benefits	Percentage of poverty line[c]
Mississippi	250	24	274	186	460	58
Alabama	250	30	280	184	464	59
Tennessee	250	46	296	179	475	60
Arkansas	250	49	299	178	477	61
South Carolina	250	49	299	178	477	61
Louisiana	250	53	303	177	480	61
Kentucky	250	57	307	176	482	61
West Virginia	250	60	310	175	485	62
New Mexico	250	64	314	174	488	62
Texas	250	73	323	171	494	63
Idaho	250	74	324	171	494	63
North Carolina	250	76	326	170	496	63
South Dakota	250	80	330	169	499	63
Georgia	250	91	341	165	507	64
Utah	253	90	343	165	508	65
Indiana	250	95	345	164	510	65
Arizona	250	102	352	162	514	65
Oklahoma	250	102	352	162	514	65
Florida	250	107	357	161	518	66
Missouri	250	108	358	161	518	66
Montana	251	111	362	159	521	66
Maine	250	122	372	156	528	67
Ohio	250	122	372	156	528	67
North Dakota	250	123	373	156	529	67
Virginia	250	125	375	155	530	67
Wyoming	250	127	377	155	532	68
Delaware	250	128	378	154	533	68
Nebraska	250	129	379	154	533	68
Iowa	250	130	380	154	534	68
Oregon	250	132	382	153	535	68
Nevada	250	136	386	152	538	68
Colorado	250	142	392	150	542	69
Pennsylvania	250	148	398	148	546	70
Kansas	250	151	401	147	549	70
Illinois	250	155	405	146	551	70
Maryland	250	165	415	143	558	71
DC	250	173	423	141	564	72
New Jersey	250	178	428	139	567	72
Rhode Island	250	203	453	132	585	74
New Hampshire	250	204	454	132	585	74

TABLE A-2 *(continued)*

State	Average federal AFDC benefit[a]	Average state AFDC benefit[a]	Average combined AFDC benefit[a]	Maximum food stamp benefit[b]	Proposed total benefits	Percentage of poverty line[c]
Washington	250	207	457	131	588	75
Vermont	311	158	469	127	596	76
Wisconsin	279	194	473	126	599	76
Michigan	272	209	481	124	605	77
Connecticut	250	243	493	120	613	78
Minnesota	278	237	515	113	628	80
New York	262	262	523	111	634	70
Massachusetts	268	268	536	107	643	82
California	289	289	578	94	672	86
Hawaii	258	223	481	247	728	74
Alaska	297	297	594	154	748	83
Average	255	136	391	151	541	69
Coefficient of variation	0.05	0.50	0.19	0.15	0.10	0.09

a. Proposed average payment for a family of three.

b. Food stamp benefits use the current funding formula, are based on average AFDC payments, and assume the standard deduction ($106 per month). Food stamps have higher maximum benefits and standard deductions in Alaska and Hawaii.

c. See table A-1.

TABLE A-3. Changes in Welfare Enrollments and Costs
If Proposed Program Had Been Enacted in 1988, by State
Costs in millions of 1988 dollars

State	AFDC families[a]	Federal AFDC costs	State AFDC costs	Food stamp costs	Administrative costs
Mississippi	6	131	2	−19	1
Alabama	5	107	2	−16	2
Tennessee	7	134	4	−20	3
Arkansas	2	36	1	−5	1
South Carolina	3	65	2	−10	2
Louisiana	9	174	6	−26	2
Kentucky	4	84	3	−13	2
West Virginia	2	38	1	−6	0
New Mexico	1	26	1	−4	1
Texas	18	368	16	−56	6
Idaho	0	7	0	−1	0
North Carolina	4	83	4	−13	2
South Dakota	0	5	0	−1	0
Georgia	5	110	6	−17	3
Utah	0	0	0	0	0
Indiana	3	62	4	−10	2
Arizona	2	38	2	−6	1
Oklahoma	2	37	2	−6	2
Florida	9	182	12	−29	7
Missouri	4	89	6	−14	2
Montana	0	0	0	0	0
Maine	0	0	0	0	0
Ohio	12	235	17	−38	3
North Dakota	0	2	0	0	0
Virginia	5	91	7	−15	4
Wyoming	0	5	0	−1	0
Delaware	1	12	1	−2	0
Nebraska	1	12	1	−2	0
Iowa	1	17	1	−3	0
Oregon	1	15	1	−2	1
Nevada	0	10	1	−2	0
Colorado	2	35	3	−6	1
Pennsylvania	6	129	11	−22	5
Kansas	1	21	2	−4	1
Illinois	15	296	27	−50	5
Maryland	4	76	7	−13	2
DC	1	20	2	−3	1
New Jersey	5	109	12	−19	5
Rhode Island	0	1	0	0	0
New Hampshire	0	3	0	−1	0

TABLE A-3 *(continued)*

State	AFDC families[a]	Federal AFDC costs	State AFDC costs	Food stamp costs	Administrative costs
Washington	1	15	2	−3	1
Vermont	0	0	0	0	0
Wisconsin	0	0	0	0	0
Michigan	0	0	0	0	0
Connecticut	0	4	1	−1	0
Minnesota	0	0	0	0	0
New York	0	0	0	0	0
Massachusetts	0	0	0	0	0
California	0	0	0	0	0
Hawaii	0	0	0	0	0
Alaska	0	0	0	0	0
Total	143	2,883	170	−456	70

a. Monthly average in thousands of families.

Index

178